EAT *like a* MAN

THE ONLY COOKBOOK A
MAN WILL EVER NEED

Esquire

EAT *like a* MAN

THE ONLY COOKBOOK A MAN WILL EVER NEED.

| *Foreword by* | *Introduction by* | *Edited by* |
| TOM COLICCHIO | DAVID GRANGER | RYAN D'AGOSTINO |

Recipes as told to Francine Maroukian   Designed by Headcase Design

Published by

CHRONICLE BOOKS
SAN FRANCISCO

Produced by

MELCHER MEDIA

Library of Congress Cataloging-in-Publication Data available.

ISBN: 978-0-8118-7741-1

Manufactured in China

10 9 8 7 6 5 4 3 2 1

Chronicle Books LLC
680 Second Street
San Francisco, California 94107
www.chroniclebooks.com

Contents

Foreword

BEING ASKED TO WRITE THE FOREWORD for a book called *Eat Like a Man* got me thinking on the subject of men and food: We all know what it means to "eat like a man," but what does it mean to cook like one? What, if anything, is unique about the way that men cook?

Sadly, I knew there'd be no way to avoid trafficking in gender stereotypes. And not because cooking like a man involves sexist clichés about our great boldness or daring; many of the most fearless and creative people I know are women. But there are a few truisms about men that do apply to cooking, so here goes:

#1. Men don't stop to ask for directions. This hackneyed old chestnut is true. We don't. But as much as this can frustrate our more sensible companions, I think it's an asset in the kitchen. Why? Because recipes are best treated as mere jumping-off points, as trailheads, so to speak, for one's culinary adventures. Don't get me wrong—a recipe can be incredibly useful as a training tool, guiding a cook through a new technique or introducing him to new flavor combinations. I taught myself to cook using Jacques Pépin's recipes. But I only started really having fun in the kitchen when I threw out the rule book and started riffing on my own.

#2. Men like to know how stuff works. We like to tinker, to build, to renovate our own bathrooms and slide with a wrench under our own cars. At our best, we bring that spirit of curiosity into the kitchen, wanting to understand the chemistry of why bread rises, a steak sears in a pan, and salt makes everything taste better. Curiosity may have killed the cat, but it has spurred many chefs on to aim higher, invent whole new methods, and solve problems creatively.

#3. Men don't always think with their heads. We all know that men can be easily led away from the path of reason given the proper motivation, and in the kitchen this can be a good thing. Any rational person would know better than to throw a match into a pan rimmed with alcohol or to roast an entire pig, hooves and all, over leaping open flames. But our occasional willingness to abandon lucid thought in exchange for an exciting possibility can lead us down a path of great creativity. To this day, my most exhilarating cooking comes when I stop thinking too hard, and just cook from the gut.

Historically, men dominated professional kitchens just as universally as women dominated domestic ones. That division is beginning to break down, with more women than ever making names for themselves in restaurant kitchens and an increasing number of men cooking at an amateur level. I know fewer and fewer guys who restrict their culinary ambitions to manning the backyard grill—a hoary cliché I'd be happy to get rid of once and for all. This is a great thing. And if you picked up this book, you're probably part of the new vanguard of men who consider cooking one of the manly arts. I support you in this! Keep up the good work, and keep on cooking like a man.

—TOM COLICCHIO

Introduction

MY DAD DOESN'T COOK MUCH. He, like me, has a few things he's comfortable making. But he doesn't cook much. Mostly, he cooks when hunger strikes him and there is no option but to take matters into his own hands. He, like me, benefits from living with a woman who sustains him, both spiritually and (to the purpose of this book) gustatorily.

But when he does decide to make something, he's both resourceful and fearless.

His granddaughters—my daughters—still talk about a shrimp chowder he threw together out of nothing one afternoon while we were all on a Carolina vacation. The ingredients he had to work with were not promising: some leftover grilled shrimp, some nonfat milk, some leftover corn on the cob, and whatever else was in the refrigerator after five days in a rental house. When I saw what he was up to, I scoffed and turned away. Neither shrimp nor corn looks like much after two days spent in plastic wrap squeezed beneath the beer and the leftover noodle salad. And, being a rental, this was a modestly equipped kitchen.

And yet . . . what he made was delicious. Fifteen minutes after he began, my daughters and most of their cousins were leaning up against the kitchen counter avidly spooning mouthfuls of chowder into their adolescent metabolisms. I don't know what he put in that pot—and I'm sure it's in no way replicable—but what he managed to do was delight and satisfy hungry people.

Which is pretty much what this cookbook is about. It's about offering you (a man, in our mind's eye, but really anyone) the skills and the confidence to delight and satisfy yourself and the people you care about. And the thing that makes this cookbook singular is that every recipe it contains is both manageable and ambitious. These are meals and dishes that are well within the bounds of (a) what men want to eat, and (b) what the moderately ambitious male cook is capable of producing in a reasonable amount of time. These recipes are sophisticated in conception but simple in execution. No special equipment is called for, any technical expertise required will be simply explained, and there'll be no straining of anything through cheesecloth.

Every recipe comes from a chef we respect. Each of these chefs was vetted and encouraged and edited by *Esquire*'s professional cook/food writer/contributing editor Francine Maroukian (who eats better and more interestingly than anyone we know). And each recipe was also tested by *Esquire*'s male editors—at home, in their modest kitchens, for their friends and families.

One of the defining characteristics of manhood is the joy we take in tangible results. We love possessing the competence that allows us to fix a broken lock, replace an electrical fixture, make minor auto repairs. This book benefits from knowledge gleaned over years by dozens of great chefs—knowledge that is condensed into recipes and instructions that will enable you to impress, to delight, and to enjoy a unique and endlessly replicable form of satisfaction: dinner. Or lunch. Or breakfast.

—DAVID GRANGER,
Editor in Chief, *Esquire*

SOME TOOLS YOU'LL NEED

THIS IS A BASIC KITCHEN INVENTORY, IN NO PARTICULAR ORDER. SOME OF THESE ITEMS YOU'LL NEED MORE THAN OTHERS. THERE ARE PLENTY OF OTHERS YOU COULD BUY, BUT THIS LINEUP WILL GET YOU THROUGH MOST RECIPES. FOR SOME ITEMS, WE SUGGEST BRANDS WE LIKE.

Recommendations by Francine Maroukian

POTS AND PANS

Not many, but definitely these:

• 10-INCH FRYING PAN

We recommend the All-Clad 10-inch Fry Pan: Pure aluminum is encapsulated between a nonreactive 18/10 stainless steel interior cooking surface and an exterior casing of polished magnetic stainless. The result is a heat-diffusing base that allows ingredients to brown. The metals are bonded together in a process called "cladding" to guarantee a level cooking surface.

• A COUPLE OF GOOD, HEAVY-BOTTOMED SAUCEPANS.

Various sizes.

• CAST-IRON PAN

Lodge, an American maker of high-quality cast-iron pans for more than a hundred years, preseasons pans in the factory (its "Logic" line). The 10¼- and 12-inch sizes, with a 2-inch depth, are most practical—any larger and, depending on the size of what you're cooking, the cooking fat could run off to the sides and burn.

• A DEEP, HEAVY PASTA POT

This can also be used for deep-frying, cooking live lobsters, making the Sunday Gravy on page 86, and even stove-top braising.

GOOD KNIVES

Not many, but definitely these:

• 9-INCH CHEF'S KNIFE

The most versatile and useful of all knives. Spend some money on this.

• PARING KNIFE

Try the Wüsthof Classic Paring Knife (with 3-inch blade): This small-bladed knife with a tapered tip is not designed for impact work like chopping. Because its size gives better control for close-up work, a paring knife is typically used off the cutting board for hand-held jobs, like peeling and coring fruit, eyeing potatoes, and trimming the ends off vegetables.

• SERRATED KNIFE

For bread, sandwiches, tomatoes, cheese—soft foods that are easily destroyed. Try the one pictured on page 75.

CUTTING BOARD

On which to cut.

BOWLS

Good to have on the counter to hold chopped onion or minced garlic or whatever until you're ready to use it. Preparing ingredients and setting them out before you start—called *mise en place*, French for "put in place"—saves time.

DUTCH OVEN

We use the Lodge Signature Series 7-quart Dutch Oven. There's no greater symbol of American down-home cooking than the almighty cast-iron pot, so good at conducting and distributing heat that you can braise, sear, fry, stew, or even roast in it, using an open-flame burner, walled oven, or even a campfire. Made by the oldest family-owned cookware foundry in the United States, this pot is preseasoned, giving it a smooth, matte-black heirloom patina right out of the box. With moderate care—no soap, just a good scrubbing with a nylon brush and then a thorough drying to prevent rust—it will last so long you can bequeath it.

OLIVE WOOD SPOON

Olive wood has a very small grain, which means you can stir and stir and the edges of the spoon will never fray, as it does with more porous wood. Unlike metal utensils, it can be used to scrape the browned bits of food stuck to the bottom of the pot without releasing tiny metal particles. Proceed to the risotto on page 168.

COLANDER

Mostly for draining pasta.

GRATER

For cheese. Can also be used for zesting citrus, although a Microplane is handy when it comes to that.

MUSIC PLAYER AND SPEAKERS

Because it's better to cook with music. Try Chill Pill speakers, which are tiny, portable, and surprisingly powerful. (chillpillaudio.com)

MEAT THERMOMETER

Powered by a 3-volt battery, the geeky Thermapen has a bright, clear digital readout, a three- to four-second response time, and remarkable temperature range (-58° to 572°F). The unique thermocouple (electronic temperature sensor) requires only about an 1/8-inch insertion of the probe, giving accurate readings for anything from a skirt steak to a rib roast.

MEAT LOAF PAN

Buy a nonstick meat loaf pan with a perforated insert that allows fat to drain away, keeping the meat crisp instead of steaming, and lets you lift your loaf out in one solid piece. It's like magic. And it will make you want to make meat loaf.

SPOONS

Keep some handy, for tasting sauces as you go.

SCALE

The thing about a kitchen scale is that you don't realize you need it until you do. More and more recipes are calling for ingredients by weight, and what you won't get at your farmers' market is a computerized receipt detailing exactly what you bought. The Oxo Good Grips scales are the easiest to use, store, and read.

STOVE

SALT DISH

Many recipes ask you to salt or season "to taste," which means adding a little at a time until it's the way you like it. A small dish of salt on the kitchen counter makes it easy to add a pinch at a time. It also looks chef-y.

THE WHIRLEY POPPER

By Scott Raab

Tens of millions of Americans think they like popcorn, even though they have no idea what popcorn tastes like. They love it nuked and crap-coated at work; they buy bags, at ball games and movie theaters, of warm packing peanuts. And this would be merely pointless and sad, like copulating with pantyhose, were popcorn—real popcorn—not the finger food of the gods.

Okay, maybe not gods. But we're talking Aztecs here, which is pretty close. Popcorn was handed down to us by the noble Iroquois and Pequot, and what do we do? Give it to Paul Newman and Orville Redenbacher, to peddle pricey sacks o' salty Styrofoam.

It doesn't have to be this way, folks. For around $25 Wabash Valley Farms will send you a hand-cranking six-quart Whirley-Pop Stovetop Popcorn Popper. Made in a barn in Indiana, it comes with a 25-year warranty. (They also sell six-pound bags of gourmet popping corn for less than ten bucks.) You put a little bit of oil in your Whirley-Pop, a half cup of corn, turn on the heat, crank—gently, you lazy bastard—for three minutes or so, and you will taste that popcorn beloved of Tlaloc, Aztec god of maize and thigh-high fertility.

Tlaloc advises adding a little garlic powder, salt, and black pepper. And cumin. Tlaloc gets ticked if you forget the cumin. (popcornpopper.com)

THINGS A MAN SHOULD KNOW ABOUT
ENTERTAINING

By Ted Allen

Planning a dinner party in a way that you're actually capable of getting it done without panicking is important. It's bad hospitality for the host to be freaked out.

Get a drink in your guests' hands within five minutes of them walking into the door. This could be Champagne, this could be a cold beer, it could be a martini, whatever. Something. When you go to a big banquet or wedding, they have waiters with trays full of glasses right by the door. It immediately sends the message, Hey, workday is done, the party is beginning, welcome to my house, rock and roll.

There is no shame in offering a selection of, say, three beverages, and that's it.

You can further make life easier for everybody by imposing a theme on the evening. Sangria night. A whiskey party. Margaritas. One main option, and then some beer and wine for people with tequila allergies.

This also helps indecisive people to get the hell out of the way so somebody else can get to the bar.

Here's the recipe for sangría, totally scalable: I bottle of white wine, 2 ounces of Cointreau or triple sec or Grand Marnier, and 2 ounces of brandy. You can also add a little honey, and then whatever fruit you like. Lemons, limes, apples, pears, grapefruit, cherries. Your call. Everyone loves sangría.

Wine: When in doubt, buy more red than white. White-wine drinkers generally don't mind switching to red; red drinkers generally do mind switching to white.

You must feed people when serving intoxicants, and you want to feed them things that are absorbent. If you like making canapés, great. I find it kind of tedious. You can't

go wrong with a whole bunch of cheese. Or antipasti. Just don't fill them up too much before dinner.

One of the biggest mistakes people make when they cook for other people is to think that it has to be fancy and elaborate. This results in enormous expense and nine days of labor, plus you end up trying to assemble a croquembouche in front of your guests and everyone's experiencing flop sweat.

Never try to pull off a dish you haven't made before.

It's okay if you finish cooking something easy after your guests arrive—some dishes must be prepared *à la minute*, as chefs say. Just remember to keep talking.

Dishes that can be made ahead for a casual party: room-temperature salads. Pasta salads, rice salads, potato salads.

There is no shame in a really good potato salad.

And then you just cook a skirt steak or something, which needs to be cooked immediately before you serve it but also cooks in two minutes a side. Boom. You're done.

If you're entertaining a senator, maybe the standards are different. But for normal humans, cook stuff people like to eat. They're not looking for a seven-course meal.

Strongly consider hiring a bartender. Absolutely worth the money, even if there are only six or eight of you. They refill drinks, they clear dirty glasses, they remember to slice the limes.

If you were to send a written invitation to your closest friends asking them over for dinner, that might be kind of strange. E-mail, call, yell it over the back fence. Even your boss—e-mail is fine.

The best dinner parties are the ones where 60 to 70 percent of the guests are established friends, and the rest are new blood.

Also consider the mix. Artists and writers in the same room as hedge-fund managers can be a wonderful thing. Not that I know any hedge-fund managers.

Of course, it falls on you to introduce these people.

My favorite size group to entertain is about six people. The conversation never dies. Having twenty people in your house is like surfing at a punk show. The next thing you know, the house is empty and all your wineglasses are dirty and you're standing there asking yourself, Why did I do this again?

And yet we do it again. Cooking for people is an enormously significant expression of generosity and soulfulness, and entertaining is a way to be both generous and creative. You're sharing your life with people.

Of course, it's also an expression of your own need for approval and applause. Nothing wrong with that.

There is no shame in a potluck.

The dinner party is one of the last places in American culture where we have ritual. There's a rhythm to it: You walk in the door, you have a drink, you have some appetizers, then you go sit down, you eat, then you have dessert and another drink—it's just a pleasant, civilized, great way to live.

There should never be dead air. Make a huge playlist, put it on shuffle. People are only going to be dimly aware of the music. It should be good and it should be cool, but they're barely going to hear it, which is as it should be.

Not everything in your music library is appropriate for a dinner party. Few people want to hear a Sammy Hagar guitar solo while they eat their soup.

A host should be aware of how much alcohol he drinks. Getting too drunk at your own party has many bad consequences, not the least of which is that you'll overcook the steaks.

People who don't drink alcohol should not be made to feel awkward. You have to have more than Diet Coke and water on hand for them. Seltzer with fruit garnishes, sparkling French lemonade—invite them to the party.

Nor should people who don't eat meat be served an afterthought of hastily dressed lettuce.

It's amazing what dimming the lights and lighting a thousand of those cheap votive candles can do for the atmosphere.

A centerpiece is equally transformative. This is easy. A bowl of apples is a great centerpiece.

Buy ice.

One thing: This should be fun. You, as the host, are supposed to have a good time too. We do this at least once a week at our place. We love to cook. We do it because it's fun and because we enjoy it; if we didn't enjoy it we wouldn't do it.

If you destroy that rack of lamb you need to be able to laugh about that and order a big mess of ziti from the Italian joint around the corner.

There is no shame in buying an apple tart and some ice cream for dessert. That's what the French do.

Ted Allen is the host of *Chopped* on the Food Network.

CHAPTER 1: BREAKFAST

Banana-Bread
FRENCH TOAST

Douglas Keane | Cyrus | Healdsburg, California

BREAKFAST AT HOME CAN BE SPECIAL without being complicated. I came up with this twist on French toast for a diner that I helped open outside Denver.

SERVES 1

DIFFICULTY:

EASY	REASONABLE	WORTH THE EFFORT

2 slices banana bread (preferably dried out)

2 large eggs

1 tbsp milk

pinch of cinnamon

1 tbsp unsalted butter

maple syrup

½ vanilla bean, split and scraped

½ tsp grated lemon zest

2 to 3 tbsp sour cream

- Start with thick—like 2-inch-thick—slices of banana bread. Beat the eggs, milk, and cinnamon until well combined.

- In a nonstick skillet, heat the butter until barely foamy. Thoroughly coat the bread with the egg mixture (dripping off excess), add to the pan, and cook about 2 minutes on each side.

- Meanwhile, warm the maple syrup with the vanilla bean—throw the seeds and the pod in with the syrup.

- Top French toast with the syrup and a big spoonful of lemon sour cream—the cool tartness will balance the sugar. (To make it, add the lemon zest to the sour cream and whip until thickened, so the cream won't just melt and fade away when it hits the hot bread.)

TIP: For a bigger batch of vanilla syrup: Split and scrape a whole vanilla bean into a can or bottle of maple syrup, close, and shake a bit. After a while, it will be ready to go.

Italian
BREAKFAST SANDWICH

Michael Symon | Lola | Cleveland, Ohio

EVERY SUNDAY MY FATHER would go into the kitchen and become Mr. Sandwich, toasting up good slices of bread and filling them with all sorts of combinations. Some were good, some horrendous. But it turned me into a sandwich junkie. When you're making a breakfast sandwich, there's no time to waste. Frying the salami—sopressata is ideal because it's generously larded—crisps up the meat and gives the sandwich body. But it's also efficient, because you use that same pan to make a sunny-side-up egg, glazing it with the spiciness of the rendered fat. (You can also use this trick to cook onions, peppers, or greens for a flavor boost with no extra work.) There's a lot going on in this sandwich, but it has great balance: The saltiness of the meat is offset by the sweetness of the basil and the creaminess of the egg and mozzarella. Soaking sliced red onion in ice water is something I learned from my mom. It takes the raw bite out of the onion and keeps it light and crunchy. This is a rich sandwich, but it's refreshing. And the beautiful thing is, it's not just for breakfast.

SERVES 1

DIFFICULTY:

EASY | REASONABLE | WORTH THE EFFORT

4 to 6 thin slices (about 4 oz) sopressata or dry-cured Italian salami

1 large egg

2 thick slices sourdough bread

2 slices (about 2 oz) prosciutto

2 thin slices (about 2 oz) fresh mozzarella cheese

2 paper-thin slices red onion, soaked in ice water for 2 minutes, then drained

4 large fresh basil leaves

- In a skillet over low heat, fry the salami until lightly crisp and fat is rendered, about 2 minutes per side. Remove and set aside.

- In the same skillet, fry the egg sunny-side up. Remove and set aside.

- On one piece of bread, layer the salami, prosciutto, mozzarella, and drained red onion; close with remaining slice. Place in the same skillet, pressing down on the sandwich with the palm of your hand, and lightly toast on both sides. Remove, open the sandwich, and layer the egg and basil on the bottom half. Close, slice on the diagonal, and serve.

Lobster

SCRAMBLED EGGS

Stephanie Harris | The Island Inn | Monhegan Island, Maine

SERVES 4

DIFFICULTY:

EASY | REASONABLE | WORTH THE EFFORT

8 large eggs

3 tbsp cream cheese, softened

2 tbsp shredded Cheddar cheese

3 oz lobster meat, chopped (fresh or frozen)

2 tbsp finely diced red bell pepper

2 tbsp finely diced yellow onion

coarse salt and freshly ground black pepper

1 tsp canola oil

- Whisk the eggs and cream cheese together well. Add the Cheddar, lobster meat, bell pepper, and yellow onion. Season with salt and pepper and combine well.

- In a large, nonstick skillet heat the oil over very low heat. Add the egg mixture to the pan and cook over low heat, stirring frequently with a wooden spoon, until cooked to desired consistency.

EGGS *and* TOMATO SAUCE

Steven Petrecca | Jones | Philadelphia

THIS DISH ALWAYS DID THE JOB of feeding my brothers and me. There was (and is) always tomato sauce in our fridge, left over from Sunday lunch. The deceptively simple combination of eggs cooking in a good, fresh sauce is heaven to me.

SERVES 2

DIFFICULTY:

1 clove garlic, crushed

3 to 4 tbsp olive oil, plus more for drizzling

two 28-oz cans whole plum tomatoes

4 large eggs

2 thick slices Tuscan bread, toasted

shaved Parmesan cheese

torn fresh basil for garnish (optional)

- Preheat the oven to 400°F. In an ovenproof sauté pan over medium heat, cook the garlic in a good amount of olive oil—3 or 4 tablespoons—until it sizzles. Add the tomatoes and crush with a potato masher. (Chunkiness is a matter of preference.) When the foaming subsides and the oil rises to the surface (the sauce glistens), lower the heat and simmer until the sauce thickens, about 45 minutes.

- To keep yolks whole, crack each egg into a small bowl and gently slide it into the hot sauce. Transfer the pan to the oven until the whites set but the yolks are still runny—a nice sunny-side-up egg—about 3 minutes. Transfer 2 eggs per person to the bread, spooning extra sauce around the bread. Top with shaved Parmesan and a drizzle of olive oil. A sprinkle of torn basil is optional but nice.

SUBSTITUTE: Without the homemade sauce, this dish suffers a bit, but you can heat 4 cups store-bought sauce instead.

Griddled
EGG-AND-BACON SANDWICH

Randy Zweiban | Province | Chicago

SERVES 2

DIFFICULTY:

EASY	REASONABLE	WORTH THE EFFORT

2 slices applewood-smoked bacon, finely diced

cracked black pepper

3 large eggs

1 tbsp sour cream

4 slices whole-wheat or multigrain bread

4 slices Cheddar cheese

sea salt

1 tbsp unsalted butter

- Start off by rendering the two nice, thick slices of bacon in a heavy skillet over medium heat. Crack some pepper over the bacon, and while it's cooking, whisk the eggs with the sour cream and ¼ cup of water in a bowl.

- Lay out the bread and top each with a slice of Cheddar.

- When the bacon is just about done, strain out the fat (saving it) and add the eggs to the pan with the bacon. Let them almost set before lightly scrambling them with a wooden spoon. When the eggs are about done, divide them onto 2 slices of the bread. Sprinkle sea salt on the eggs and then cover them with the other 2 slices of bread and cheese.

- After wiping out the pan with a dry cloth, add some of the bacon fat and the butter to the pan over low heat and place the two sandwiches in the pan. Cover and let them cook for about 4 minutes, until they are golden brown, then flip them over for another 4 minutes. When the cheese is melted, they're done. Only one pan from start to finish.

EGG-SANDWICH MOMENTS

By David Granger

Ingredients: **7 eggs, scrambled; 9 slices Oscar Mayer center-cut bacon; salt; pepper; 3 toasted Thomas' English muffins, buttered.**

Prepared: **My kitchen.**

Consumed: **In Perlin's old Porsche, on the way to the Catskills, 5:30 ayem.**

Verdict: **"There's a lot of love in that sandwich."**

Ingredients: **2 scrambled eggs and bacon on a roll; salt, pepper, ketchup. Two times.**

Special ingredient: **The griddle at the Croton Mini Deli, on which every conceivable meat product has sizzled.**

Consumed: **With Chopper, overlooking the Hudson River. June.**

Verdict: **"That's the best fucking sandwich ever."**

Ingredients: **Bacon, egg, and cheese on a roll. Twice.**

Prepared: **For my daughters.**

Consumed: **Kitchen table.**

Sweetest words ever spoken: **"Dad, you want half my sandwich?"**

Conclusion: **In the history of the world, there has never been a bad egg sandwich.**

SCRAMBLED EGGS

with Smoked Salmon, Caviar, and Potatoes

Daniel Boulud | DB Bistro Moderne | New York City

BREAKFAST IS AN EASY thing to take for granted. We throw it together, we eat it quickly. That's why breakfast in bed is so romantic. It requires forethought. To pull it off, one has to get organized. Go to the farmers' market and get everything you need. You want your woman to stay lazy while you bring it to her. The food should be luxurious: scrambled fresh eggs, caviar, smoked salmon, potatoes. And if you serve it to her unexpectedly, there might be, shall we say, compensation.

SERVES 2

DIFFICULTY:

EASY | REASONABLE | WORTH THE EFFORT

½ lb thin-skinned potatoes about the size of golf balls

5 large eggs, at room temperature

coarse salt and freshly ground black pepper

2 tbsp unsalted French butter or crème fraîche

2 tsp very thinly sliced fresh chives

1 tsp grated lemon zest

¼ lb sliced smoked salmon

1½ oz caviar (golden osetra)

- Timing is everything. Prepare the potatoes, caviar, and salmon before starting the eggs. The smooth, creamy consistency of the eggs comes from constant whisking.

- Put the potatoes in a small pot with cold water and a pinch of salt and cover. Bring to a simmer over medium-high heat and cook until tender. Check doneness by piercing with the tip of a paring knife. Keep the potatoes in the water until ready to drain and serve—this keeps the skin from drying out. Set aside.

- Prepare a double boiler: Add about 2 inches of water to a medium-sized pot and bring to a simmer. Crack the eggs into a stainless steel bowl and whisk until thoroughly mixed. Season generously with salt and pepper, then place the bowl on top of the pot, leaving about 1 inch of clearance between the bottom of the bowl and the simmering water. Using a small rubber spatula or wooden spoon, stir the eggs in zigzag patterns. If eggs begin to coagulate too fast, lower the heat. When small curds appear, switch to a whisk and gently stir the eggs, scraping the bottom of the bowl as much as possible. When the eggs take on a porridgelike texture (soft but not soupy or runny), remove the bowl from the heat and stir in 1 tablespoon of the butter or crème fraîche, the chives, and lemon zest. Put the eggs into serving dishes.

- Drain the potatoes, split and toss with remaining butter or crème fraîche, then top with smoked salmon and caviar.

LOVE,

OR

SCRAMBLED EGGS

TO SOME PEOPLE, BREAKFAST MEANS SUSTENANCE.
TO OTHERS, IT MEANS EVERYTHING.

By Scott Raab

REAKFAST IS BREAKFAST. No metaphor, no symbol—save maybe in the sense that any social custom mirrors every other social custom, which is to say that either everything is a metaphor or symbol, or that nothing, especially not so fine and free a thing as breakfast, is. Breakfast is too good to screw it up with meaning.

And yet I miss the eggs, by which I mean I miss my wife. She took a job a year ago with an outfit known for grinding its people to the bone. She gets up at 4:30 A.M. and works often past 7:00 P.M., with no benefits, no holidays or vacation—if she doesn't work, she isn't paid—and she tells me she likes it. I don't know why. The money's nice, but we did fine before. She says the job "validates" her.

Me, I figure she just finds it easier to deal with the job than with me. The eggs are collateral damage. Anyway, she never ate them herself, and now they're over. No more eggs.

It was only a couple of mornings a week, tops, and generally iffy—she'd overwhisk them and they'd stiffen up, or keep them on the heat too long, or I'd suddenly crunch on a speck or two of eggshell—but I never said no, never turned them down. Not once.

I don't know why, or why I miss them, or why I don't just scramble some myself. I mean, I always liked the color and the smell of them, at least until they started browning, but there was nothing Proustian about them; the only thing my mother made for breakfast was heartache. It's not as if my wife and I sat and ate the eggs together, either, but it also didn't feel like she was serving me. At least not to me.

Sometimes I'll point out to her—I'm big on pointing things out to her, she's even bigger on ignoring me, and marriage, by the way, is no metaphor, either, and both of us working at home is no recipe for bliss—that there used to be eggs, and if she's paying attention, she'll say, "All you have to do is ask," and I'll say, "I didn't used to have to ask." And then she goes back to her laptop and I make a sandwich.

Like I said, the eggs were iffy. But they were hot, and pale yellow, and her offering them felt—forgive me—something like love. Not storybook: workaday love. The real thing.

Those scrambled eggs, they validated me. Us.

GREEN EGGS

and Parma Ham

Evan Funke | *Rustic Canyon* | *Santa Monica, California*

SERVES 1

DIFFICULTY:

EASY	REASONABLE	WORTH THE EFFORT

1 English muffin

2 thin slices Parma prosciutto

2 tbsp unsalted butter

2 large eggs

sea salt and freshly ground black pepper

about 1 tbsp smooth pesto

- Split and toast the English muffin and top each half with a thin slice of prosciutto.

- In a small nonstick skillet over low heat, melt the butter; it should not froth. Crack the eggs into the pan—the eggs shouldn't crackle or spit on contact; that would mean your heat is way too high—and cook over low heat until the whites are settled but yolks are still runny, 3 to 4 minutes. Once the whites look soft and white, gently spoon the melted butter in the pan over the yolks until hot, about 1 minute. This will help cook the eggs from top to bottom and keep the yolk silky but warm. Season with salt and pepper, and transfer the eggs to the English muffin. Spoon a nice smooth pesto over the eggs. Not the chunky, jarred pesto—the smoother stuff from the refrigerator or freezer case. It's better.

SUBSTITUTE: With this recipe, you don't have to think too much. If you don't have prosciutto, use Black Forest ham. No English muffins? Try sourdough toast.

HOW TO
FORAGE
LIKE A MAN

WE GAVE A CELEBRATED CHEF AND MOLECULAR GASTRONOMIST NINE MUN-
DANE INGREDIENTS AND ASKED HIM TO COOK A MEAL—NO SPECIAL EQUIPMENT
OR TECHNIQUES. IT'S A SKILL WE ALL HAVE, JUST TO VARYING DEGREES.

By Wylie Dufresne

Chef | wd-50

IT'S A CLASSIC EXERCISE: Cooks are given a number of ingredients and told to make a menu. My sous- chef and I used to sit around at the end of the night having beers, and someone would challenge: "Go into the cold-appetizer fridge and see what you can make." You grab some pickled onions, some corned duck, some celery, and suddenly you're halfway to a great sandwich. You can take any ingredient and do something you're comfortable with; you just have to think for a second. The recipe below has some versatile tricks to tuck in your pocket. A few basics of instant entertaining:

1. Breakfast has a big window of appeal, so that's always a good place to start. You can serve it all day, and then again when it gets really late.

2. Start in the pantry, not the fridge. You might find half a roasted chicken in the fridge that somebody bought at the grocery store yesterday, but you have to know what's in the cupboards to give it flavor. Even the most die-hard bachelor has old spices lying around, and smoked paprika from five years ago is better than nothing.

3. Think about what you like. Wings? Okay, take mustard, honey, and hot sauce—guys always have hot sauce—and you've got sauce. Serve it with roasted pulled chicken. But when you serve it, you don't have to present it as your take on hot wings. You don't have to say, "Look, sweetheart, I re-created what I had at ESPN Zone last night."

THE PANTRY

EGGS | BACON | BEER | KETCHUP | COFFEE | PASTA (ANY SHAPE)
POWDERED CHEESE (FROM MAC-AND-CHEESE BOX) | POTATOES | PICKLES

THE RESULT

BREAKFAST FOR DINNER

BACON EMULSION

Render 3 or 4 slices of bacon in a sauté pan and save the drippings. Coarse-chop the bacon and place in a blender with a little bit of water and blend on the highest speed. Add a few splashes of beer (the better the beer, the less you need) and drizzle in some of the bacon fat, which will emulsify the mixture. Adjust the seasoning with a little salt and ketchup.

COFFEE COUSCOUS

Brew some strong coffee. Cook your pasta of choice, here Israeli couscous, in the coffee using the measurements on the box. If using couscous (recommended), add the coffee in bit by bit, as you would with a risotto. Stir in a spoonful or two of powdered cheese.

POACHED EGGS

Crack an egg for each person into individual cups and slide eggs into barely simmering water. Poach for 3½ minutes, then carefully remove with a slotted spoon and place in a bowl of ice water.

POTATO-PICKLE HASH

Dice a potato per person and sauté in the pan with a few tablespoons of olive oil until crisp. Take off the heat, salt and pepper to taste, and fold in some pickles, diced small.

To Serve

Reheat the poached eggs with a little warm water if they were prepared ahead of time and then drain. Smear some of the bacon emulsion in the center of each plate and top with a small pile of the coffee couscous. Put an egg alongside the couscous and add some of the potato-pickle hash. Dust some of the powdered cheese around the plate, but not too much.

PANCAKES

Ryan D'Agostino | *Food Editor,* Esquire

MY BROTHER CAN WALK INTO any kitchen and cook up something good—really delicious—using whatever ingredients he finds. No cookbook, no grocery-store run. Somehow, he comes up with a bouillabaisse or risotto or crème caramel. I don't have this skill, but I wish I did. So in my wallet, I carry a recipe for pancakes. I have used it countless times to whip up fluffy, sweet flapjacks, and my hosts always react the same way: with surprise, appreciation, and pronouncements of my prowess in the kitchen. Not long after we started dating, I made a particularly good batch in my wife's tiny Manhattan apartment. Her dog loved them and, in turn, me—and getting a woman's dog on your side is never a bad thing. Last summer, I made some at a waterfront house in Maine where we were guests. We were recently invited back, and our hosts asked if I could add blueberries this time. As a display of gratitude, a meal you've created beats a bottle of wine every time. It doesn't have to be pancakes, although they're good because most people have the ingredients. If you carry around any good, simple recipe, it shows you have thought ahead about pleasing others. Plus, like a .38 tucked into your belt, a recipe in your wallet lends confidence. Once, at a friend's place in Los Angeles, there was no maple syrup. After four seconds of panic, I began foraging for some sort of topping. What I came up with was a concoction of ingredients I found in the kitchen: strawberry jam, butter, confectioners' sugar, mint leaves, and a drop of lime juice. It blew them away.

SERVES 4

DIFFICULTY:

EASY	REASONABLE	WORTH THE EFFORT

CAN BE DOUBLED, TRIPLED, ETC.

www.schlosshotel-kronberg.de — info@schlosshotel-kronberg.de

Pancakes

1 egg

1¼ c. flour
2½ tsp. baking powder
2 Tbl. sugar
¾ tsp. salt

1¼ c. milk
3 Tbl. melted butter

Combine dry. Beat egg. Combine wet.
Mix wet into dry. Stir until barely mixed.

BREAKFAST-STYLE RED BEANS AND RICE GRITS

with Eggs and Andouille

Lee Richardson | Ashley's | Little Rock, Arkansas

RED BEANS AND RICE WAS TRADITIONALLY a "cupboard dish" made on Monday using Sunday's ham bone: a big pot left on the stove to simmer while the laundry was done. It's always better the next day, and for that reason, it makes a fine and fortifying breakfast. A man about his game should be able to pull a bag of last week's beans out of the freezer, heat them up, and top them off with a couple of loose sunny-side-up or poached eggs and a piece of grilled andouille sausage. As a local boy, I don't stray far from New Orleans customs in cooking a dish like this. But short on grits one morning, I had to improvise, using my spice grinder (simply an inexpensive coffee grinder reserved for this use) to mill some rice and then cook it up grits style. A man's gotta make do.

SERVES 6

DIFFICULTY:

1 lb dried red kidney beans, picked over

4 cups chicken stock

1 onion, chopped

3 stalks celery with leaves, chopped

1 green bell pepper, seeded and chopped

6 cloves garlic, chopped

½ lb good-quality smoked ham, diced

1 lb smoked ham hocks

1 bay leaf

2 tbsp Creole seasoning

2 tbsp Lea & Perrins Worcestershire sauce

1 tsp Tabasco sauce

1 dozen turns freshly ground black pepper

3 tsp coarse salt

Rice Grits (recipe follows)

12 poached or loose sunny-side-up eggs

grilled andouille sausage for serving

chopped scallion greens for garnish

- Put the beans and 8 cups water in a small stockpot over high heat and bring to a boil. Remove from the heat, cover, and let soak for 30 minutes.

- Drain the water from the beans and add 8 cups fresh water and the stock, along with the onion, celery, bell pepper, garlic, ham, ham hocks, bay leaf, Creole seasoning, Worcestershire sauce, Tabasco sauce, and black pepper. Bring to a boil, then reduce to a simmer; cook for 90 minutes. Add the salt and crush some of the beans with a potato masher. Continue to simmer for 30 minutes. Remove the ham hocks, strip off and return any meat to the pot, and keep the beans warm.

- At this point, you can remove half the beans, cool, and freeze for future use.

- Ladle about 1 cup beans into each serving bowl and top with about ½ cup rice grits. Top the grits with poached or fried eggs and serve with a piece of grilled andouille and some freshly chopped scallions.

RICE GRITS

1 cup long-grain white rice

1 tsp coarse salt

3 tbsp unsalted butter

- In a clean coffee grinder or small food processor, grind the rice into a meal.

- Bring 4 cups water to a boil with the salt and 1 tablespoon of the butter. Slowly whisk the rice meal into the boiling water and continue to whisk until the mixture begins to thicken and spit at you. Lower the heat and continue to stir for about 3 minutes. Cover, reduce heat to low, and cook until thick and creamy, about 15 minutes. Stir in the remaining 2 tablespoons butter.

CONTINUED FROM

WHAT THE 21ST CENTURY
WILL TASTE LIKE

A PREVIEW OF WHAT YOU'LL BE EATING FOR THE REST OF THE CENTURY.
HOPE YOU LIKE PORK. HOPE YOU REALLY LIKE VEGGIES.

By David Chang

Chef | Momofuku

Recently I was chatting with one of my purveyors about meat, prices, and the food chain. Michael raises Tamworth pigs in upstate New York and rocks his John Deere cap without a trace of irony. He's an honest, upright citizen, a real person, not some revolutionary or back-to-the-land type. So it really chilled me when he said, "America better prepare for some uncomfortable changes. Things might get really ugly."

You've seen the articles, right there on the front page next to equally uplifting stories about oil, the economy, and the war: The cost of food—of producing and procuring it— is soaring. In the restaurant world, it's all anyone can talk about. And the thing is, this is no temporary spike; it's actually a massive correction.

Ever since my parents came to America in 1968, it has been meat and milk 24/7. They emigrated from war-ravaged Korea and, like Americans coming out of World War II, they couldn't believe—and didn't resist—the Crazy Eddie abundance of the American agricultural industry. As far as my parents are concerned, meat grows on trees.

But guess what? The machinery that's pumped so much meat into our lives over the last half century was never built to last, and now it's breaking down big-time. Feed is more expensive. Gasoline is more expensive. Milk, rice, butter, corn—it's all going through the roof. And for the foreseeable future, it's not coming back down. Farmer Michael's feed costs have risen 400 percent in the last twelve months. To make a profit on the beautiful turkeys his family is raising in time for Thanksgiving, he'll have to charge a hundred bucks a bird. At Momofuku, I'm paying 150 percent more for humanely raised pork belly than I was paying at this time last year. And at the hyperglobal megachains that feed most of America, the only way they'll be able to keep selling one-dollar hamburgers is to grow their "protein units" in petri

dishes, add even more filler to their products, and outright enslave the workers whose backs they're already breaking to keep costs artificially low.

It's depressing, this state of affairs, and sometimes I let myself wallow in it. But then I think about the opportunity this situation presents. Let's allow these harsh new realities to force us to do something that Alice Waters has been advocating for decades: Let's finally embrace the truth that food is not something to be taken for granted. As a culture, we need to be more curious about where our food comes from. We need to buy from farmers who are trying to do things the right way. We need to think before we eat.

If we do, we'll find that our cuisine and eating habits will more closely resemble those of the nineteenth century than the late twentieth. Hunting will be less about the buck points and more about the meat. Nose-to-tail eating will make a comeback—not because of fashion or Fergus Henderson (whom I love), but because of scarcity and price. And small-scale farming—little vegetable gardens in the backyards of homes in cities, suburbs, and the countryside alike—will become not just economically sensible but cool. Hell, maybe foraging for mushrooms and wild fruits will become a seminormal skill again.

At the table, this means our plates will be heavier on grains and greens, and meat will shift from the center of the dish to a supporting role—the role it's played throughout history in most of the world's cuisines. At Momofuku, we've made a name for ourselves selling lots of pig and not accommodating vegetarians. So, yeah, I recognize the hypocrisy of me—Captain Fucking Pork Bun—telling you to eat more veggies and less meat. Guilty as charged. But don't get me wrong: My restaurants still won't kowtow to vegetarians. We will, however, focus more on vegetable and grain dishes in which meat adds flavor, not heft. Like the one on the next page.

GRITS

with Fried Farm Eggs, Pickled Scallions, Red Ball Radishes, and Salted Ham Scraps

David Chang | Momofuku | New York City

SERVES 2 HUNGRY PEOPLE (3 OR 4 NOT SO HUNGRY)

DIFFICULTY:

EASY | REASONABLE | **WORTH THE EFFORT**

1 cup coarse white grits, such as Anson Mills brand

3 cups Ham Stock (recipe follows)

3 cups water

3 tbsp unsalted butter

coarse salt and freshly ground black pepper

1 bunch red ball radishes with green tops attached

½ cup country ham scraps (shavings and fatty pieces from the outside of ham), plus scraps reserved from making stock (see Note)

4 large locally farmed eggs

8 Pickled Scallions (recipe follows)

½ handful arugula

- Cook the grits in the stock in a saucepan, covered, over low heat, stirring every 10 minutes or so, until the grits are thick and the spoon stands upright. Gradually stir in water, about ½ cup at a time, and cook until grits are creamy and tender (but not mushy) and hold their shape on a spoon, about 1½ hours. To finish, uncover the pan and vigorously stir in 2 tablespoons of the butter. Add salt and pepper to taste.

- While the grits are cooking, trim the radish greens and wash well. Slice the radishes and set aside in a bowl with the greens. Put the ham scraps in a frying pan with the remaining butter and crisp them up. Set aside, then fry the eggs in the same pan.

- Ladle the grits into a shallow bowl. Add the fried egg and garnish with radishes and radish tops, pickled scallions, arugula, and ham scraps.

  NOTE: Try Benton's Country Ham. It's the best country ham out there. (bentonshams.com)

HAM STOCK

¼ cup country ham scraps

½ tsp cracked black pepper

3 tbsp soy sauce

1 small onion, coarsely chopped

- In a small pot, combine the ham, pepper, and soy sauce; add 5 cups water and bring to a slow simmer for about 1 hour. Add the onion and cook another 30 minutes. Strain the stock, reserving ham pieces that are free of skin.

PICKLED SCALLIONS

1 lb scallions, trimmed

1 cup rice vinegar

1 cup sugar

1 tsp fine salt

pinch of Japanese seven-spice or freshly ground black pepper

- Rinse the scallions well and place in a large heatproof bowl. Combine all the remaining ingredients in a pot with 2 cups of water, bring to a boil, then pour over scallions. Let cool to room temperature. Place in a jar with a tight lid and store in refrigerator for a week before eating.

NOTE: You can also pickle baby leeks this way, or, if you're making the dish in the spring, ramps.

WHAT I'VE **LEARNED** THOMAS KELLER

CHEF, YOUNTVILLE, CALIFORNIA

Interviewed by Ryan D'Agostino, 2010

I always have peanut butter around.

One of the biggest mistakes I think chefs make are portion sizes. Too much.

Try to sit down and eat a thirty-two-ounce steak. It's hard.

What boys learn from sports is teamwork. And not getting upset when you lose. Although we always did get upset.

God to me when I was seven or eight was: fear—of going to hell, of going to the reformatory. Or of getting your hand slapped by the nuns.

Having four older brothers was great because nobody in the neighborhood was allowed to beat me up. "There's my big brother over there. You wanna start some shit with me?" But my brothers would beat the crap out of me.

You have to have music. When we started the French Laundry and there were just three of us in the kitchen, our go-to music was the sound track to *Reservoir Dogs*. The beat, you know, it just gets you pumped up. "Little Green Bag." We went through so many copies, because somebody would get so tired of it that at the end of the night they'd throw it in the frying oil. We'd have to buy a new one.

Time and temperature. It's all about time and temperature.

Everybody says, "I created that." Well, what do you mean you created that? Something inspired you, something led you down that path, something pushed you forward and you discovered it. You realized it, you put it together, but did you really create it?

Awareness, inspiration, interpretation, evolution. Or not—maybe there are no evolutions. Maybe that's just it.

You can get on the phone and get a case of potatoes in. But if you were out there digging it, cultivating it, weeding it, harvesting it, it's like, well, I'm going to really take care of this potato.

You get a job, you get a place to live, and you survive.

A good friend is somebody who persistently tries to get you to spend time with them.

Everything begins with the quality of the product.

A sandwich has always been about the bread. Toasting it is important to me, because you not only have a textural contrast, you also have a temperature contrast. But a good sandwich is such an individual thing. A good sandwich could be toasted peanut butter and jelly.

I had really enjoyed just sitting with my father later in his life, not even saying anything. Just being around him.

I don't want to open a restaurant that's only good for five years. What's the legacy in that?

No one's gonna do it for you.

I've eaten fried ants in Mexico and grasshoppers in Thailand, which are fine. I'm not sure I could really get into a goat's eye. I don't think I'd eat a big grub off of a tree. If I was starving, sure.

I always wanted a Porsche when I was a kid. Well, I bought one in 2000. It sits in the garage.

Restaurants, to me, are sanctuaries for people to go to.

There's no better reference point in comfort for me than a beautiful roasted chicken. It has that aroma that is so captivating. You cook it in one roasting pan with vegetables, so you have kind of a one-pot meal. You have to use specific techniques—you want to hydrate the skin so it gets that golden consistent, crispy skin; you want to be able to temper it, so you learn how to temper things, you understand the importance of heat on food, and how to adjust from high temperature to low temperature. You understand the internal temperature of the bird and where you're willing to compromise, because the breast may be a little more done than the leg, but if we brine the chicken, then you know, learning what brining does to food, penetration of seasoning as well as maintaining moisture—you have a lot of techniques there, and you have something that you can go back to, year after year, season after season. So I think that would be the first thing that I would teach somebody who doesn't know how to cook.

Eggs are the perfect food.

Scrambled. What do I do? I just scramble the eggs. Whisk them together, a little salt, a little olive oil in the pan. I don't get my eggs too hot. Really, really, slow. Take them out just before they're done. I eat them with Ak-Mak crackers.

PULLED BABY-BACK RIBS

Eggs Benedict

Raymond Chen | Inn at West View Farm | Dorset, Vermont

SERVES 2

DIFFICULTY:

| EASY | REASONABLE | WORTH THE EFFORT |

lcftover meat from cooked ½ rack baby-back pork ribs, shredded

Bull's-Eye hickory smoke sauce

hoisin sauce

2 slices corn bread (from a mix, if you'd like)

2 large eggs

2 tsp distilled white vinegar

sliced scallions for garnish (optional)

cracked black pepper

- On our days off, I often eat leftovers. This is one of my favorite breakfasts. Preheat the oven to 350°F. Take the half rack of ribs (enough for 2)—we make ours with a Memphis rub and our own sauce, but you can buy pretty good cooked baby-backs—place it on a roasting pan, heat it in the oven for 10 minutes, and then shred the meat off the bone.

- Meanwhile, make hickory-hoisin sauce: I've used Bull's-Eye hickory smoke sauce and hoisin sauce (preferably Lee Kum Kee's), mixed in a 2-to-1 ratio, with great success. Toss the meat in the sauce—not a lot, since the corn bread is sweet—and set it on top of a couple slices of corn bread. (Betty Crocker has a nice mix. I heat and butter the pan before adding the batter, which gives the bread a nice brown-butter flavor and a toasted exterior.)

- Poach a couple of eggs by gently cracking them into a pot of aggressively simmering water with the vinegar. After about 2 minutes, remove the eggs with a slotted spoon and place on top of the pork. Finish with some scallions, if you have any, and cracked pepper.

ESQUIRE
Classics

PRETTY EASY RECIPES FOR SOME OF THE BEST BREAKFAST DISHES OF ALL TIME.

Reprinted from the *Esquire Cookbook*, 1955

OMELET À LA MARECHIARO

As featured on ships of the Italian Line.

For 4, beat 6 eggs, add 3 tablespoons heavy cream, salt and pepper to taste, a pinch each of basil and parsley, I ounce grated Parmesan cheese. Heat a large frying pan and put in it I ounce of butter and I tablespoon olive oil; heat until it smokes, then pour in the egg mixture. Remove pan from heat and add: 7 ounces thin-sliced mozzarella cheese and 3 ounces cooked ham (sliced or diced). Cook 4 ounces fresh, sliced mushrooms quickly in butter and add (or drain and add a 4-ounce can of broiled-in-butter sliced mushrooms). Squeeze over the mixture a trifle of lemon juice. Now sprinkle the top with I ounce grated Parmesan cheese and I ounce melted butter. Place in hot oven for 5 minutes. Slide the omelet onto a hot platter and serve at once, garnished with sprigs of parsley.

HAM AND EGGS HAWAIIAN

...from Trader Vic's, Oakland, California

For each person, grill or fry I center-cut slice of ham until done. (A 1/2-inch slice of tenderized ham will take about ten minutes for each side; better cut gashes in the outside fat to keep the ham from curling up under the broiler heat.) Meantime, make a syrup of I tablespoon brown sugar, I teaspoon butter, and a pinch of salt; cook together in a small pan until hot and thickened. Peel and split I ripe banana; fry it in butter until brown. Keep hot while you fry, in the same pan, 2 slices canned pineapple. Add more butter to the pan, lower the heat, and fry 2 country-fresh eggs gently. Arrange ham, eggs, and fruit on a hot platter with French fried potatoes, toast, or toasted English muffins. Pour the syrup over the ham and fruit and rush to the table.

More Egg Ideas:

● Add Parmesan cheese and fines herbes to scrambled eggs.

● A drop of Tabasco sauce added to a soft-boiled egg gives it character.

● Diced chives and crumbled smoked cheese blended with eggs makes a superlative omelet.

● A drop of herb vinegar in the butter makes fried eggs sit up and smile.

● Pop an egg in an individual casserole that has been lined with partly cooked bacon and bake until egg sets. A few drops of caper sauce and 3 or 4 capers atop each egg will vary the flavor.

● Poach eggs in beer for something special in taste and texture.

● Fry eggs over low, low heat in plenty of butter—and baste them with the butter from time to time until done to taste.

● Serve fried eggs "beurre noir": While eggs are gently frying, brown a little butter in another pan. Add finely chopped fresh parsley, a dash of good vinegar, coarse salt, and freshly ground black pepper. Put eggs in individual ramekins and pour the sizzling butter over them.

CORNED BEEF HASH

Mix 2 parts chopped corned beef with I part chopped boiled potatoes and a little chopped onion. Season with a little freshly ground black pepper (corned beef probably doesn't need salt). Melt a bit of butter in a frying pan, spread the corned beef mixture in the pan and cook until well browned, then fold as you would an omelet. Transfer to plates, place a poached egg on top of each serving, and serve immediately. The same technique works with other cooked meat, too.

Bacon-and-Egg

FRIED RICE

Jet Tila | Wazuzu in Encore at the Wynn | Las Vegas

ONE OF MY FAVORITE BREAKFASTS IS BACON AND EGGS—but cooked into fried rice. It's a one-and-done—everything I love on one plate. There's always leftover rice after you order takeout, and that cold rice is perfect for cooking fried rice on a home stove. It doesn't stick to the pan, so you don't have to use much oil.

SERVES 1

DIFFICULTY:

EASY | REASONABLE | WORTH THE EFFORT

1 tsp low-flavor, high-smoke-point oil, such as canola

4 slices bacon, chopped

2 large eggs

2 cups cooked rice (leftover takeout is fine)

pinch of coarse salt and freshly ground black pepper

1 to 2 tbsp oyster sauce

chopped scallions

- Heat the oil in a skillet until it's very hot. Add the bacon and cook until it's crisp. Scoop the bacon to one side and tip the skillet so the fat and oil pool. Crack the eggs into the fat and allow them to settle a bit and pick up some browned edges before scrambling, so you get some of those caramelized fried-egg bits. Use a spatula to beat down on the eggs (like a drum) to break the yolks. When the eggs begin to tighten (but before the yolks get hard), use the edge of the spatula to chop them into dime-sized pieces.

- Fold in the rice—that is, instead of stirring, use a scooping motion, lifting the rice from the bottom to the top. Using the flat side of the spatula—not the edge; it's bad juju to break rice grains—press down in a circular motion (like you're giving someone a massage) to combine the ingredients. Once the rice starts to dry out a bit, hit it with the salt and pepper and the oyster sauce to pull all the flavors together. Right before serving, fold in lots of chopped scallions so the steam opens up their flavor without wilting them. Crisp is good.

Resuscitated
PIZZA

Mathieu Palombino | Motorino | Brooklyn

SERVES 1

DIFFICULTY:

EASY		
	REASONABLE	WORTH THE EFFORT

1 handful grated Parmesan or Gruyère cheese

1 slice leftover pizza

2 slices bacon

1 large egg

extra-virgin olive oil for drizzling

- Preheat the oven to 450°F. Sprinkle the Parmesan or Gruyère—or any *real* cheese you have—on a slice of leftover pizza. Place the pizza on a baking sheet or aluminum foil and put it in the oven for a few minutes, until the cheese starts to bubble.

- Meanwhile, sauté the bacon in a pan over medium heat. When it's done, remove, crumble, and reserve the bacon. Drain the excess fat from the pan, but don't wipe it down. Crack the egg into the same pan and cook sunny-side up. Top the pizza with the bacon, then the egg. Drizzle with high-quality olive oil.

FISH *and* GRITS

Ria Pell | Ria's Bluebird | Atlanta

SERVES 2

DIFFICULTY:

| EASY | REASONABLE | WORTH THE EFFORT |

two 8-oz fish fillets (red snapper, tilapia, or catfish)

1 jar blackening seasoning

Creamy Grits (recipe follows)

2 handfuls shredded white Cheddar cheese

toasted baguette for serving

- Heat a cast-iron skillet over medium-high heat for about 10 minutes.

- Dip the fish fillets in the blackening seasoning—we make our own, but good ol' Paul Prudhomme's from the grocery store is fine—that's been spread out on a plate or pie pan. Coat both sides if you want it spicy. Carefully place in hot skillet, seasoned-side down, cover, and cook for 1 to 2 minutes. Flip and cook about 2 minutes more—the fish should be white, flaky, and not opaque when cooked through.

- Dish up two proper-sized bowls of grits, sprinkle with the Cheddar, and top each with a fillet of fish. Serve with toasted fresh baguette for maximum enjoyment.

CREAMY GRITS

coarse salt

2 cups slow-cooking grits

1 tsp salted butter

¼ cup half-and-half

¼ tsp freshly ground black pepper

- Bring 6 cups salted water to a boil in a medium saucepan. Slowly stir in the grits and reduce the heat to a low simmer and cover. Cook for 20 minutes, stirring frequently with a wire whisk. Turn off and stir in the butter, half-and-half, and pepper, then set aside.

Jalapeño-and-Ancho
OATMEAL

Edward Lee | 610 Magnolia | Louisville, Kentucky

THIS SPICED-UP OATMEAL TAKES ME BACK to my childhood, when I would belly up to my favorite Korean rice gruel flavored with sweet soy sauce and chile peppers. Oatmeal, for me, is like Occidental congee, so naturally I like to take my Irish oatmeal and unleash its spicy alter ego.

SERVES 2

DIFFICULTY:

EASY	REASONABLE	WORTH THE EFFORT

½ cup steel-cut oatmeal, preferably McCann's

1 dried ancho chile, seeded and finely chopped

2 large spoonfuls almond butter

1 banana

honey to taste

small handful of dried cherries

pinch of coarse salt

brown sugar to taste

pinch of cinnamon

Hungarian paprika

½ cup unsweetened coconut milk, plus more for drizzling

1 Granny Smith apple, cored and sliced

jalapeño chiles, finely chopped

- I bring the oatmeal and 2 cups of water to a simmer for about 20 minutes undisturbed, while I rummage through my pantry for flavor. I've never made it the same way twice, but the general plotline goes like this:

- At about the 20-minute mark, I deseed the ancho chile, chop it fine like confetti, and throw it in. Next, I add the almond butter, the banana, which I smash disgracefully into the oatmeal, two seconds of a stream of honey about the thickness of a pencil, a child's handful of dried cherries, a pinch of salt, a nugget of brown sugar, a dusting of cinnamon, and as much Hungarian paprika as you can hold with three fingers.

- When the oatmeal is tender but still chewy, it's done—about 25 minutes' total cooking time. I thin it out with about ½ cup of coconut milk and top each serving with a little more coconut milk, a slice of Granny Smith apple, and—best for last—some jalapeño chile chopped fine, seeds and all. (I use a whole one on mine.)

THOSE PARTS

By Tom Junod

EATING HEARTS. AND BRAINS. AND MAYBE BALLS.

My wife was making her own granola when the box of organs arrived. She was baking it, and the house smelled nutty, sweet, toasty, beyond reproach, the way Eden must have smelled before God got pissed and Adam got hungry. The organs changed that. They had been shipped from a New York butcher who was either laying down some kind of gauntlet—eat *this*, omnivore—or figured anybody with a hunger for organs deserved no better treatment than the organs themselves. The box was cardboard, the kind you usually get mail-order apples in, but what I saw when I flipped open the flaps was nothing less than a biohazard: a big plastic bag full of lamb hearts, another full of lamb kidneys, and another full of lamb balls, as well as a half-dozen little white cardboard boxes, two lamb brains to a box. There was no ice, and the bags were not sealed, not even knotted, and as the frozen organs thawed, they'd begun to bleed, the kidneys in particular, since one of the peculiarities of eating organs is that while hearts aren't all that bloody, kidneys are inexhaustibly so, each one a little kidney-shaped artesian well of gore. They'd also begun to smell, for reasons that need no elaboration here. Instantly, the house stopped smelling like granola—essence of innocence, tinctured with blamelessness—and started smelling like an old-folks' home, and Man's Fall from Grace was enacted yet again, by nothing more than our indiscriminate appetites.

But the smell, sudden and encompassing as it was, wasn't even what freaked me out. Nor the kidneys themselves, nor the hearts, nor even the brains, because they at least behaved themselves, staying in the bloody bags and the tiny damp boxes. The balls didn't. The balls were slippery, literally more than metaphorically. Two balls had already escaped from the ball bag when I opened the box, and they kept on escaping, like an unwelcome jackpot, until the box was teeming with the soft, silky, glistening things, each one of them about the size and shape of an ostrich egg and threaded with squiggly blue veins. The veins are what freaked me out. They are what introduced me to the uncomfortable intimacies of organ meats, otherwise known as offal. I have often heard people say that they draw the line at eating innards, with the explanation that it's akin to cannibalism. I have never shared their squeamishness, for once you start killing animals built along the same bilateral lines as you are and feasting on their flesh, it seems a little late for lines to be drawn. I mean, why *now*? Why not just eat the core along with the rest of the apple? But I recognized the blue veins winding their way through the forcibly disembodied sheep junk. I had never seen my liver or my kidneys or my heart or my brain or my thymus gland, which would be sautéed as sweetbreads. I had, however, seen my balls—they aren't innards; they're *outards*—and they looked just like these, allowing, of course, for discrepancies of scale. Indeed, my balls bore about the same relation to these, size-wise, as the pitiable little lamb brains presumably bore to my own superior bean, which reminded me that all human hunger boils down to the same remorselessly evolved sense of license—that if your balls are bigger than your brains, we reserve the right to put both on our plates, along with everything else.

My dad used to cook kidneys on Sunday mornings. Never a churchgoer, he would wake up early and sauté the kidneys in a black cast-iron pan with a lot of salt and butter. The smell would make my brother sick, but I would get out of bed and follow it downstairs, led by my nose like a cartoon wolf. I would sit at the table in my pajamas and watch my father as he fried eggs in the browned butter, and then poured some water and salt in the pan and boiled it down to a brown sauce, which he would pour over the kidneys and the eggs. Then we would eat, sopping up the juices with pieces of unbuttered toast that became brown and soggy, and to this day nothing evokes the memory of childhood hunger like a pan smoking with the smell of butter and piss.

So I have been an offal eater all my life. When I was in college, I recognized a kindred spirit when, in *Ulysses*, James Joyce writes that "Leopold Bloom ate with relish the inner organs of beasts and fowls. . . . Most of all he liked grilled mutton kidneys which gave to his palate a fine tang of faintly scented urine." This is more than an offhand remark about the nature of Bloom's appetite; it is the first thing Joyce writes about him, and his way of casting Bloom in opposition to his other wandering hero, the proud intellectual Stephen Dedalus. What Bloom eats characterizes him as humble and earthy, and so it's ironic that over the last few years, offal has become Dedalus food instead of Bloom food—it's become food that people who are interested in food are *supposed* to like, while at the same time the people who used to like it don't eat it anymore. It's no longer poor people's food; it is, for one thing, expensive, and even in my hometown, Atlanta, two high-end restaurants have sprung up to sate the presumed hunger for the parts of the body hidden to all but veterinary surgeons. At one, the charmingly named Abattoir, a waitress even elevated the pronunciation of the word: It used to be *oaf*-full, but she pronounced it something like "Oh, Fall," which is what the devil whispered in paradise.

The promotion of offal has even become the kind of "trend" that is either celebrated or lamented among people who cogitate excessively over what the body instinctively knows—i.e., "foodies." But they can cogitate all they want, because it doesn't matter if you're *supposed* to like it: You have to like it to eat it. You're either able to swallow it, or you have to spit it out. You either

> The veins are what freaked me out. They are what introduced me to the uncomfortable intimacies of organ meats, otherwise known as offal.

have a hunger for it, or you are repulsed, and for the same reasons. There's something forbidden about it, something secret by the body's own designs and therefore taboo: It's the other dark meat. Oh, we proudly fatalistic chophouse habitués say that we eat the flesh of the beasts of the earth, but we don't, really; we only nibble at the margins, bloody as those margins may be. A steak, after all, is pure carapace—a vestige of the skeletal system, what's left of the animal's armor, and there are many cuts of meat the animal could conceivably do without, for a little while anyway. But offal is the essence. It's what rib eyes and mutton chops are designed to serve, and to protect. It's the body's secret stash, hidden away, and often it must be extricated: The chef at Abattoir doesn't get his veal brains in a box or a bag but rather in the skull of a calf, which he must open with a hacksaw, laboriously, three per half hour. The depth of flavor, as the foodies say, comes from the depth of the organ inside the animal, its privileged position beyond flesh and bone. One is tempted to say that offal is the pearl of the slaughterhouse, but really it's the oyster: the shellfish of the body, strong in taste, rich in nutrients, toxic in cholesterol content, and really, really *soft*.

The softness is the problem with offal, and the allure. Let's face it: When we're speaking of eating organs, half the time we're eating glands, and they give the mouth the opposite of a firm handshake. Indeed, we cook skeletal meat to tenderize it; we cook offal to firm it up. We brine; poach; pat dry; then sear in a pan or under a broiler, so that it turns brown and loses some of its smoothness and pallor, each of which are as disagreeable, in their way, as the lack of tooth. And yet no matter what we do to offal, it is never anything other than what it is, because the questions it poses are abstract and cannot be answered in the simplicity of the kitchen. Our qualm when eating skeletal meat is what it might have run through—the grasses, the meadows, the fields. Our qualm when eating organ meat is what might have run through it. That is why kidneys and brains are the most challenging—and hence the most delicious—of all the offal: because we know. Liver? For most of us, it remains undefined, and so it's the hamburger of innards. Sweetbreads? I dunno—do we even have a thymus gland, or is it, like the appendix, a vestigial extravagance? But kidneys and brains are the seats of excrescence and cogitation, respectively, and so make us human . . . and so they raise the question of whether they do the same to lambs and calves. Our most terrible thought, when preparing and eating brains, is whether they, in fact, contained thoughts, contained consciousness, contained soul. We cook food to transform it, but brain, by human prejudice, resists transformation and remains a replica of what it is, a Matchbox car of the miracle of mind. I cooked my tiny boxed lamb brains in brown butter until they curled a little at the corners, then splashed them with vinegar and scattered them with capers, but when I sliced them, I'd seen those slices before, in CAT scans and autopsy photos. Plus, they were soft, so soft that cookbooks call them "delicate," so soft they were "creamy," and not in a good way—in a smegmatic way. I ate them in solitude, digested them with difficulty, and spared my family the lonely spectacle.

The kidneys, though: They respond to heat the way fresh oysters respond to lemon, recoiling a bit, tightening, moving, as if to prove they're still alive. In times of exigency, we say of our own kidneys that they are "bursting," and the kidneys of lambs and calves behave burstingly under the influence of flame, plumping and sizzling even as they exude their unmistakable tang. Oh, Lord, what a tang—since half the kidneys the butcher sent me were black and eye-wateringly fragrant, I probably shouldn't have eaten any of them. But I couldn't resist. I was making pasta for my family, with cauliflower, garlic, and bread crumbs. I threw one on-the-turn kidney under the broiler, and then another, then another, and ate with such pleasure that my daughter asked for a taste. I gave her one, as my father had given one to me, as a kind of creaturely communion. She spit it out instantly, reflexively, like Agassi's return of serve. "It tastes like pee," she said, and after she finished her paradisiacal pasta, she went to the refrigerator for dessert and spied the unruly bags of balls. "Are these the brains, Daddy?" she asked.

"Kind of," I said, and the next morning I threw them away, because I had no idea what do with them, and besides, you have to draw the line somewhere.

My Father's Sunday-Morning
HEATHEN BREAKFAST

Tom Junod, Esquire *magazine*

SERVES 1

DIFFICULTY:

| EASY | REASONABLE | WORTH THE EFFORT |

kidneys (however many you want, however many you can stand—same thing, really)

milk to cover

olive oil for frying

salt and freshly ground black pepper

butter for frying

eggs

white bread, toasted, unbuttered, for serving

- Soak the kidneys in enough milk to cover them for a day or two. They'll still be bloody—don't worry about it. Halve them, lengthwise. See that white thing? That you do have to worry about. Cut the spokes that connect it to the kidney with a knife. Throw away and banish from your thoughts. Cut the kidneys crosswise now into pieces like thumbs.

- Heat a cast-iron skillet. Medium-high. Splash in a little olive oil, not too much. When it shimmers, it's ready. Add the kidneys in one layer—in batches, if necessary. Salt and sauté till they sizzle, till they brown, till they move. Don't overcook, but don't heed cookbooks that tell you to serve medium-rare. People will freak out. Salt again, and grind some pepper over the pan. When all the kidneys are nice and browned at the edges, add butter. Don't be shy with it. It will sort of explode and brown fast. Remove the pan from the heat before the butter starts smoking and burning.

- Remove the kidneys and fry some eggs in the butter. When the eggs are done, place on a plate with the kidneys.

- Splash some water in the pan and work off the kidney bits with a spatula. Keep cooking at high heat until the sauce is brown and a little thick. Add more salt, if your heart can stand it. Pour the sauce over the eggs and the kidneys and mop it up with the toast. And sing. You have to sing while you're cooking this. If you don't sing, it doesn't work.

FRENCH TOAST BLT

with Roasted Garlic Vinaigrette

Sue Zemanick | Gautreau's | New Orleans

THIS COMBINATION OF two all-time favorites is based on our New Orleans–style egg-soaked-and-fried *pain perdu,* or "lost bread," a traditional method used to reclaim bread that was growing stale. I use fresh challah—thickly sliced or it will fall apart during the soak—because it has a rich sweetness but airy texture from being kneaded. The long soak creates a custard that cooks into the bread so it puffs up in the oven after getting a crisp crust in the frying pan. That's your base, topped with the saltiness and smokiness of bacon with a good cure, ripe tomato, and peppery arugula.

SERVES 6

DIFFICULTY:

EASY | **REASONABLE** | WORTH THE EFFORT

12 thick slices smoked bacon

2 cups heavy cream

5 large eggs

coarse salt and freshly ground black pepper

6 slices challah bread, at least I inch thick

2 tbsp canola oil

2½ cups grated Gruyère cheese

12 slices ripe tomatoes (about 3 small)

6 cups arugula, cleaned

Roasted-Garlic Vinaigrette (recipe follows)

- Preheat the oven to 350°F. Place the bacon on a rimmed baking sheet and bake until crisp, 10 to 15 minutes. Leave the oven on.

- Combine the heavy cream and eggs in a bowl and whisk to thoroughly blend. Season the mixture with salt and pepper to taste. Soak the bread in the mixture for 15 minutes, then turn the slices over and soak for an additional 10 to 15 minutes.

- Place a nonstick skillet over medium heat. Add the canola oil. Once the oil is hot (it will shimmer slightly), fry the challah slices on each side until golden brown, working in batches. Transfer the challah to a baking sheet and place in the oven. Bake until the custard is cooked through, 6 to 8 minutes; the bread should soufflé, or puff up. Remove from the oven, cover each slice with grated cheese, and return the pan to the oven to melt the cheese. Once the cheese is melted, about 4 minutes, remove from the oven. Put 2 slices bacon and 2 slices tomato on each slice of challah and drizzle with some of the vinaigrette. Toss the arugula with the remaining dressing (or enough to coat) and place atop each piece. Serve warm.

ROASTED-GARLIC VINAIGRETTE

3 heads garlic

olive oil for drizzling

2 tbsp sherry vinegar

1 tsp Dijon mustard

coarse salt and freshly ground black pepper

- Preheat the oven to 375°F. Slice the tops off the garlic so the cloves are exposed. Place the heads in a baking dish and drizzle with olive oil. Cover the pan with foil and roast until the garlic is golden brown and fragrant, 20 to 25 minutes. Remove the garlic from the oven. Cool briefly before squeezing the cloves out of their skins into the bowl of a blender. Combine the vinegar and mustard, blending until smooth. With the machine running, slowly drizzle in ¾ cup olive oil. Keep the blender running and season with salt and pepper.

BUCKWHEAT FLAPJACKS

Wolfgang Vomend | Bavarian Inn | Shepherdstown, West Virginia

SERVES 4

DIFFICULTY:

| EASY | REASONABLE | WORTH THE EFFORT |

2 large eggs

1 cup whole milk

2 cups buckwheat flour

¼ cup all-purpose flour

1 tbsp baking powder

2 tbsp sugar

1 tsp coarse salt

unsalted butter, melted

- In a large bowl, whip the eggs and the milk together until fully mixed. In a separate bowl, sift the buckwheat flour, all-purpose flour, baking powder, sugar, and salt. Mix the wet ingredients into the dry ingredients until just barely mixed. Allow some lumps to remain.

- Heat a well-seasoned or nonstick griddle or skillet over medium heat. Brush with butter and ladle in ¼ cup of the batter. Cook until golden brown on the bottom and bubbles form on the top, about 2 minutes. Flip and cook until brown on the other side. Serve hot.

THE COFFEE MATRIX

A SIMPLE GUIDE TO YOUR IDEAL CUP

We are not scientists. We are simple people who want to make a good cup of morning coffee in our own kitchens. To that end, we designated three bean categories—specialty coffee, commuter coffee, corner-store coffee—using standard blends from three brands. Then we used five typical brewing methods, judging each resultant cup on its own merits. Somewhere below is the cup for you. —Francine Maroukian

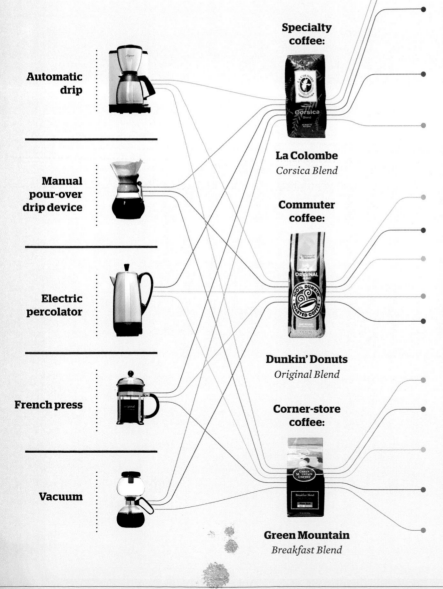

Automatic drip

Manual pour-over drip device

Electric percolator

French press

Vacuum

Specialty coffee:

La Colombe
Corsica Blend

Commuter coffee:

Dunkin' Donuts
Original Blend

Corner-store coffee:

Green Mountain
Breakfast Blend

Taste:

Smooth. Doesn't give up any flavor, even when you add cream.

Almost perfect. Something's missing, like watching full-screen instead of wide-screen. Note: Pour a small amount of hot water over the ground beans to evenly saturate them, and then add the rest.

A little tinny on the first sip, which some people like. That old-fashioned percolating noise is oddly comforting, but the coffee gets very hot.

So rich and thick, it's almost like hot dark chocolate; big caffeine liftoff. Note: Using a chopstick, stir the ground-coffee/water mixture to maximize the flavor bloom before steeping.

Second to steep-brewing in flavor. Good caffeine bump. But it takes a while—what do you drink to steady your hands while you're waiting?

Slightly watery, like what you get when you order an Americano in Europe. This is simply caffeine delivery.

Clark Kent coffee: mild and unassuming.

New England road-trip coffee: better with milk and sugar, which somehow enhance Dunkin' coffee's inherent nuttiness.

Dark and tasty, without too much oomph—for easing into your day.

Needs the doughnut on the side. Not a great match between method and bean.

Mom-and-pop coffee. Gets you going, but you may need seconds.

Rich but not too thick. Surprisingly pronounced flavor, somehow with no lingering aftertaste.

Tastes slightly "cooked," like cowboy coffee, which alters the flavor—not necessarily in a bad way.

Breakfast blend indeed—great with food. A safe, solid, crowd-pleaser, like steak medium-rare.

This method draws out the essence of even a mild bean like this.

CHAPTER 2: LUNCH

CHICKEN-PARM HERO

with Sausage

Harold Dieterle | Perilla | New York City

I EAT AT LEAST one sandwich a day. When I was opening my restaurant, I'd walk around Greenwich Village at lunch, trying all different kinds. One day, in the window of Faicco's Pork Store, I saw a pile of golden fried chicken cutlets on a massive plate lined with grease-stained paper towels and I thought, This is the place. Now I'm there twice a week. The chicken-parm sandwich is a beautiful concept, because it has all the right textures: toasty bread, crisp chicken, gooey cheese. But you've got to commit to doing it right. Baking the chicken won't work; you need the action of the frying oil to get the bread crumbs the right texture. Jarred sauce is another trap. People think making your own is a huge undertaking, but it's actually pretty easy with good-quality canned crushed tomatoes. Simmer everything for half an hour and you're set. That's it. That's the sauce.

SERVES 1

DIFFICULTY:

EASY **REASONABLE** WORTH THE EFFORT

1 boneless, skinless organic chicken-breast cutlet (about 8 oz)

2 tbsp all-purpose flour

1 large egg, lightly beaten

½ cup seasoned bread crumbs

canola or peanut oil for frying

soft semolina hero roll with sesame seeds, ends trimmed, split

Tomato Sauce (recipe follows)

2 tbsp grated pecorino cheese

¼ cup shredded buffalo mozzarella cheese

- Dredge the chicken breast in the flour (knocking off excess), dip in the egg (dripping off excess), and press in the bread crumbs (the chicken must be thoroughly coated at each step).

- In a sauté pan over medium to high heat, heat ¼ inch of oil. When a pinch of breading sizzles on contact, fry the breaded cutlet (lowering the heat if necessary) until golden brown and cooked through, about 3 minutes on each side. (Check for doneness by making a tiny cut in the thickest part of the breast.)

- Preheat the broiler. Place the open roll on an aluminum-foil-covered sheet pan and lightly toast under the broiler. Remove, and preheat the oven to 350°F. Lightly coat both bread halves with sauce and arrange a cutlet on bottom half, cutting to fit if necessary. Top with the sauce, pecorino, and buffalo mozzarella. Transfer to oven until cheese is melted, 2 or 3 minutes. Set top in place and serve.

TOMATO SAUCE

¼ cup crumbled loose spicy Italian sausage

2 cloves garlic, minced

1 cup minced white onion

2 tsp fennel seeds

2 fresh basil leaves, chopped

one 14.5-oz can crushed organic tomatoes

coarse salt and freshly ground black pepper

• In a medium saucepan over low to medium heat, cook the sausage. Drain off the fat, add the garlic, onion, fennel seeds, and basil and cook until softened. Add the tomatoes and simmer over low heat until thickened, about 30 minutes. Season with salt and pepper.

Makes about 2 cups.

Catfish

SLOPPY JOE

Rick Moonen | RM Seafood at Mandalay Bay | Las Vegas

I GREW UP IN a large family in suburban New York. My parents both worked, but my mom still had to cook for ten on a daily basis: seven kids, my grandmother, my dad, and herself. On week-nights she'd make sloppy joes, my died-and-gone-to-heaven meal: Martin's potato rolls (although a burger bun will suffice) stuffed with sticky sweet-sour joe mix, served with salty potato chips and crunchy sour dill pickles. (Come to think of it, it was probably also Mom's favorite meal because it's a one-pot thing, making cleanup very easy.) One of my first jobs after culinary school was in Key West. I learned all about cleaning and cooking seafood and found it a natural fit for my love of water. In this sandwich, use a mild, meaty fish, like U.S. catfish or tilapia, that stands up to the barbecue sauce and vegetables in texture and flavor. To preserve the taste and sweetness of the fish, opt for a thick tomato-based barbecue sauce (as opposed to vinegar-based) that goes easy on the smokiness. You'll get a tangy dish that appeals to everyone at the table.

SERVES 2

DIFFICULTY:

8 oz skinless catfish (or tilapia) fillet, cut into 1/3-inch dice

coarse salt

1/4 cup canola oil

1 small onion, diced (about 3/4 cup)

1 small green bell pepper, seeded and diced (about 3/4 cup)

2 tsp paprika

1 cup barbecue sauce

unsalted butter, softened

2 oversized burger buns (or other soft rolls), split

- Season the catfish with salt. Heat a medium skillet over medium-high heat. When the pan is hot (a drop of water will sizzle on contact), add the oil, onion, and bell pepper. Cook, stirring often, until the vegetables begin to soften, about 3 minutes. Stir in the paprika and cook, stirring constantly, for 1 minute. Add the catfish and cook for 1 minute, stirring frequently so all sides of the fish come in contact with the hot pan. Stir in the barbecue sauce and bring to a simmer. Reduce heat to low and simmer until thick, 10 to 12 minutes.

- Butter the buns and lightly toast, buttered-side down, in a skillet. Fill the buns and serve hot.

Stuffed

MEAT BREAD

Dennis Leary | The Sentinel | San Francisco

WHEN I'M AT THE STOVES, I rarely have time to eat a plate of food from start to finish, so lately I've commissioned my girlfriend to make me this sandwich every few days, and I just eat sections of it when I need to.

SERVES 2 OR MORE

DIFFICULTY:

EASY		
	REASONABLE	WORTH THE EFFORT

1 baguette (with thin crust)

deli meats and cheeses

marinated vegetables

- Preheat the oven to 350°F. Take a large, airy baguette, cut off the ends, and carve out as much of the insides as you can using a long, skinny knife or the handle of a wooden spoon. Then take whatever you like from the deli counter—prosciutto, ham, salami, some provolone, marinated vegetables—and jam everything in there with the spoon handle. Fire the whole thing in the oven for about 15 minutes and slice it up.

The
SANDWICH GLOSSARY

BRESAOLA:
Air-cured, spiced lean beef, served thinly sliced.

FICELLE:
French for "string," a longer, thinner baguette.

GHERKIN:
A small type of cucumber used for pickling.

GIARDINIERA:
Chopped vegetables dressed with oil and vinegar, often used as a condiment on Italian beef sandwiches.

GRASS:
A sandwich topper of shredded iceberg lettuce with oil, vinegar, salt, and pepper.

KNOBLEWURST:
Beef sausage flavored with garlic and eaten like a hot dog.

MORTADELLA:
A large, finely ground pork salami, studded with fat and peppercorns and occasionally pistachios and olives.

PEPERONATA:
A rustic, cooked pepper mixture, sometimes with tomatoes, onions, garlic, and olive oil, often layered into sandwiches.

PORCHETTA:
Slow-roasted boneless pork, seasoned with rosemary, fennel, and garlic.

SABLEFISH:
A fatty white fish from the Pacific Northwest. When smoked, sablefish is known as smoked black cod.

STEAK SANDWICH

Lee Hefter | WP24 | Los Angeles

A SANDWICH SHOULD be thoughtfully laid out, with components that add up to a complete meal, but the most important thing is that the ingredients should be of excellent quality. They should also be easy to come by: It's a sandwich, after all. That's why I start with steak. It's never been easier to buy great beef. For the perfect steak sandwich, don't be afraid to buy a nice cut of beef. The three basic cuts I use to make a sandwich without requiring the tenderization process of a marinade are rib eye, New York strip (sirloin), and filet, all available from any butcher. To season it, simply salt and pepper the meat, and that's it. That's all you have to do to it. This open-faced sandwich is a bit more elegant than one you might pick up at a deli; it's like a great steak salad on toast. Again, other than salt and pepper, there's no need for seasoning. You get all the zing you need from glazing the sautéed vegetables with a little steak sauce added right to the pan. Everything you want is already in that bottle—the tomatoes, the spices, the vinegar—and in just the right proportions. It's a fail-safe way to add flavor; you're going to look like a genius.

SERVES 1

DIFFICULTY:

EASY | REASONABLE | WORTH THE EFFORT

one 8-oz prime New York strip or rib-eye steak or filet mignon

coarse salt and freshly ground black pepper

2 tbsp unsalted butter, plus softened butter for roll

$\frac{1}{2}$ cup half-moon-sliced red onion

$\frac{1}{2}$ cup pickled cherry peppers (hot and sweet), sliced

1 cup thinly sliced white mushrooms

2 tbsp steak sauce, such as A.1.

1 hoagie-style soft roll, ends trimmed, split

Garlic Mayonnaise (recipe follows)

4 slices Vermont white Cheddar cheese (about 4 oz)

fresh arugula, washed and spun dry

red-wine or light balsamic vinaigrette

one 2-inch piece fresh horseradish root, peeled

- Grill, broil, or pan-sear the steak until medium-rare, season with salt and pepper, and let rest before thinly slicing.

- Preheat the broiler. In a sauté pan over medium heat, melt the 2 tablespoons butter until lightly browned, and caramelize the onion. Add the peppers and mushrooms and cook, flipping frequently, until well mixed, about 3 minutes. Add the steak sauce and simmer to glaze, about 2 minutes. Season with salt and pepper.

- Lightly butter the roll and lightly toast in the skillet (buttered-side down). Spread the toasted sides with garlic mayo and place on

aluminum-foil–lined baking sheet. Top with the cheese and melt open-faced under the broiler. Remove and transfer to a serving plate. Arrange the steak atop the broiled bread, overlapping the slices slightly, and evenly distribute the vegetable mixture, finishing with arugula dressed with vinaigrette. Using the small-hole side of a box grater or a Microplane zester, grate the horse-radish root (as when working with raw chiles, do not touch your eyes) over the sandwich and serve.

GARLIC MAYONNAISE

2 cloves garlic, peeled (or more or less to taste)

pinch of coarse salt

¼ cup mayonnaise

freshly ground
black pepper

pinch of minced fresh
flat-leaf parsley

• Place the garlic cloves on a clean work surface. Using the broad side of a chef's knife, crush slightly, using circular motions, until it becomes a paste. Add the salt and mix. Stir the paste into the mayonnaise, adding pepper and parsley.

CROQUE MONSIEUR

David Myers | Comme Ça | West Hollywood

THE SIMPLEST DISHES ARE often the most important ones—both for diners and chefs. To me, that's the croque monsieur: bread, ham, cheese, and béchamel all toasted together to make the ultimate ham-and-cheese. I can remember my first one: It was 1996, and I was on my first trip to France to apprentice at the elegant Château Les Crayères in Reims. I bounded off the plane, ready to take on Paris. Good plan—but I didn't speak much French and got lost. Then I realized I was missing a bag. Needless to say, I wasn't in the best mood. I wandered into a café and ordered a croque monsieur and a beer. That first bite was a wave of happiness. It hit all the right notes—saltiness from the cheese, smokiness from the ham, the crunch of the toast offset by the creamy béchamel. You can't go wrong with the basics: a quality French- or Italian-style loaf of bread (not baguette), good Gruyère (the Franche-Comté is best), and a decent cured ham, like Black Forest. Sure, you can dress it up—add peppered bacon or play around with different types of bread— but I'm not so sure that any of that will make this classic any better. That's one of the secrets to being a good cook: You have to know when to leave well enough alone.

SERVES 2

DIFFICULTY:

EASY | **REASONABLE** | WORTH THE EFFORT

1 tbsp butter, plus softened butter for bread

1 tbsp all-purpose flour

¾ cup whole milk

pinch of freshly grated nutmeg

coarse salt and freshly ground black pepper

2 tbsp freshly grated Parmigiano-Reggiano cheese

¾ cup shredded Gruyère cheese, preferably Franche-Comté (about 3 oz)

4 slices French or Italian loaf bread

softened butter

Dijon mustard

6 oz thinly sliced ham (about 6 slices)

• Preheat the oven to 350°F. In a small saucepan over low heat, melt the 1 tablespoon butter until foamy. Add the flour and cook, whisking constantly until smooth, about 2 minutes. Slowly add the milk, stirring constantly, and cook until the mixture thickens enough to coat the back of a spoon, about 2 minutes. Remove from the heat and season with nutmeg and salt and pepper to taste. Stir in the Parmigiano-Reggiano and 2 tablespoons of the grated Gruyère. Set the béchamel sauce aside.

- Lightly and evenly butter the bread slices on both sides and toast both sides in a sauté pan over low heat until just golden brown. Spread one side of each toasted slice with mustard. Evenly place the ham slices and about ½ cup Gruyère cheese on two of the bread slices. Top each with one of remaining bread slices, mustard-side down. Spread béchamel sauce to cover the top of each sandwich (crusts, too). Sprinkle evenly with the remaining Gruyère cheese. Place on a baking sheet and bake for 5 minutes, then place under a lit broiler until the cheese mixture on top is bubbling and lightly browned, about 3 minutes.

TIP: Cover the edges of the bread with the béchamel or they can get a little too crisp in contrast to the rest of the sandwich.

WHAT I'VE LEARNED JULIA CHILD

ICON, SANTA BARBARA, CALIFORNIA

Interviewed by Mike Sager, 2000

Fat gives things flavor.

People are uncertain because they don't have the self-confidence to make decisions.

The measure of achievement is not winning awards. It's doing something that you appreciate, something you believe is worthwhile. I think of my strawberry soufflé. I did that at least twenty-eight times before I finally conquered it.

Playing golf with men can throw off your stroke.

I'm all for hunger among the well-to-do. For comfortable people, hunger is a very nice quality. For one thing, it means you're healthy. And I love the anticipation.

Being tall is an advantage, especially in business. People will always remember you. And if you're in a crowd, you'll always have some clean air to breathe.

There is nothing worse than grilled vegetables.

Celebrity has its uses: I can always get a seat in any restaurant.

I was faced by my nieces and good friends and told I shouldn't drive my car anymore. Actually, I find I'm not quite as alert as I used to be, and it would be awful to kill somebody. So now I don't drive, and it is real hell, because you can't rush down to the store and get a bunch of parsley if you have the whim, or do something like that. It's just awful not driving, because you have to depend on other people. You get used to it, though. They have a bus here—I haven't tried it yet, but I shall.

A cookbook is only as good as its poorest recipe.

I hate organized religion. I think you have to love thy neighbor as thyself. I think you have to pick your own God and be true to him. I always say "him" rather than "her." Maybe it's because of my generation, but I don't like the idea of a female God. I see God as a benevolent male.

Tears mess up your makeup.

I'm awfully sorry for people who are taken in by all of today's dietary mumbo jumbo. They are not getting any enjoyment out of their food.

Moderation. Small helpings. Sample a little bit of everything. These are the secrets of happiness and good health. You need to enjoy the good things in life, but you need not overindulge.

I went into a doctor's office the other day and all the people—you know, the nurses and the receptionists and even the patients—were sort of short-tempered and not very nice. And it made me think, I just want to bop them over the head. It's terribly important to keep a good temper.

I don't eat between meals. I don't snack. Well, I do eat those little fish crackers. They're fattening, but irresistible.

If you're in a good profession, it's hard to get bored, because you're never finished—there will always be work you haven't yet done.

The secret of a happy marriage is finding the right person. You know they're right if you love to be with them all the time.

The problem with the world right now is that we don't have any politicians like Roosevelt or Churchill to give us meaning and depth. We don't have anyone who's speaking for the great and the true and the noble. What we need now is a heroic type, someone who could rally the people to higher deeds. I don't know what's to become of us.

You must have discipline to have fun.

Drama is very important in life: You have to come on with a bang. You never want to go out with a whimper. Everything can have drama if it's done right. Even a pancake.

I don't believe in heaven. I think when we die we just go back to the great ball of energy that makes up the universe.

Hell only exists on earth, when you've made mistakes and you're paying for them.

I don't think about whether people will remember me or not. I've been an okay person. I've learned a lot. I've taught people a thing or two. That's what's important. Sooner or later the public will forget you, the memory of you will fade. What's important are the individuals you've influenced along the way.

Always remember: If you're alone in the kitchen and you drop the lamb, you can always just pick it up. Who's going to know?

TUNA MELT

Rob Evans | Hugo's | Portland, Maine

A TUNA SANDWICH is a great, inexpensive way to eat fish. But tuna packed in water cannot compare to the flavor offered by good-quality imported Italian tuna packed in virgin olive oil. So dense and chunky it can actually look like pulled chicken, canned tuna in oil delivers a rich, meaty taste, particularly when mixed with a quality mayonnaise, like this one: I use a soft poached egg because it reduces the amount of oil necessary and produces an almost velvety texture. While the runny yolk can be smoothly emulsified, the whites stabilize the mayonnaise. This mixture can actually be gently warmed without breaking down, used as a sauce on cooked fish, or served as a dipping sauce for fried potatoes. The bits of charred rosemary add earthiness to the mayonnaise, giving it some depth. But the trick is balancing the fattiness with the natural acidity of fresh lemon juice—that's what keeps it from becoming boring or too heavy. The flavor difference will leave people wondering why your sandwich is so familiar yet so much better than anything they remember.

SERVES 2

DIFFICULTY:

EASY | **REASONABLE** | WORTH THE EFFORT

8 oz Italian tuna packed in olive oil, drained, with I tbsp oil reserved

Charred-Rosemary Mayonnaise (recipe follows) to taste

2 tbsp finely diced celery hearts

½ tsp celery seeds

coarse salt and freshly ground black pepper

4 slices multigrain bread

4 slices Gruyère cheese (about 4 oz)

unsalted butter for toasting

- Gently flake the tuna and place in a stainless steel bowl. Fold in the desired amount of mayo, chopped celery, and celery seeds, adding salt and pepper to taste.

- Lay the bread on a work surface. Spread the tuna on two slices and layer with the Gruyère. Top with the remaining bread slices and press lightly with the palm of your hand to bring the tuna just to the edges of each sandwich.

- Melt a small amount of butter in a skillet over low heat and toast sandwiches until the cheese melts and the bread is golden brown, about 2 minutes on each side. Transfer to a cutting board and cut in half on the diagonal. Serve immediately.

CHARRED-ROSEMARY MAYONNAISE

2 sprigs fresh rosemary

1 tsp distilled white vinegar

1 large egg

2 tbsp freshly squeezed lemon juice

1 tsp Dijon mustard

¾ cup extra-virgin olive oil

reserved tuna oil (from above)

- Lightly char the rosemary (hold the stems with tongs and rotate through a burner flame for about 10 seconds), strip the leaves, and finely chop (yields about 1 tablespoon).

- Bring 4 cups water to a boil, reduce to a simmer, and add the vinegar. Crack the egg and ease it into water, cooking until the white sets but the yolk is still runny, about 2 minutes. Transfer the egg (as dry as possible) to a blender or food processor with the lemon juice and Dijon mustard. Slowly add the oils, processing until thick and creamy. Add the rosemary.

Makes about 1 cup.

RICH-BOY

Kevin Davis | Steelhead Diner | Seattle

I GREW UP IN A Cajun family in southern Louisiana. Traditions ran deep, and we met at different houses for meals three or four times a week: gumbo, fried catfish, chicken stew, boiled crawfish and crabs. Even though I've laid down my roots in Seattle, I find ways to bring my old world here. There's a lot of Louisiana in this sandwich, because it starts with chaurice, a fresh, spicy Creole-Cajun pork sausage, like an uncured version of Spanish chorizo. Once the meat is out of the casing, it's easy to form patties that are the perfect size for the bread. Traditional po'boy bread has a light, crisp crust and an airy center. Also, when you order a po'boy in Louisiana, you'll be asked what you want on it, and the common answer is "dressed"—mayo, pickles, tomatoes, and lettuce. I spice up the mayonnaise with another Louisiana specialty, Crystal hot sauce. It's relatively mild and lets you add enough to get that vinegar zip without making it too hot.

SERVES 2

DIFFICULTY:

4 links chaurice (Mexian chorizo) or spicy pork sausage (about ½ lb)

unsalted butter, softened

soft French-style long loaf of bread, split and cut into 2 (6-inch) lengths

Hot Sauce Aioli (recipe follows)

iceberg lettuce, shredded

1 large ripe tomato, thinly sliced

coarse salt and freshly ground black pepper

1 dill pickle, sliced lengthwise into long "planks"

- Halve the sausage links horizontally, remove the meat from casing, and flatten into long patties. (You will have 4.) In a skillet over medium heat, fry the patties until cooked through and browned on both sides, 6 to 8 minutes.

- Lightly butter the bread and lightly toast in the skillet (buttered-side down). Spread the bread (upper and lower halves) with aioli. Arrange the sausage patties on bottom half (2 per sandwich) and layer shredded lettuce, tomato slices (seasoned with salt and pepper to taste), and dill-pickle planks on the top half of the bread. Close the sandwiches and press down lightly with the palm of your hand to flatten them in place.

HOT SAUCE AIOLI

4 large egg yolks

pinch of coarse salt

squeeze of fresh
lemon juice

1 clove garlic, minced

2 tsp Louisiana-style
hot sauce (or to
taste), preferably
Crystal

1 cup canola oil

• Put all the ingredients except the oil in a blender or food processor and blend to combine. Slowly add the oil, processing until thick and creamy.

Makes about 1 cup.

MATERIALS

By Francine Maroukian

1
ZINGERMAN'S BREAD
A white-wheat mix made with a sour starter, Zingerman's farm-loaf bread has a crisp crust and textured interior. Up to the task of transporting any sandwich filling, no matter how high you pile it. 888-636-8162; zingermans.com

2
HAM I AM'S HICKORY-SMOKED AND PEPPERED BACON SLICES
Made from Western cut (or square) pork belly, Ham I Am's hickory-smoked and peppered bacon slices are uniform and won't curl when you cook them. The hickory-and-black-pepper punch—sweetened by a roll in brown sugar—makes for a better BLT. 800-742-6426; hamiam.com

3
CLEVELAND STADIUM BROWN MUSTARD
Fiercely loyal fans are not just being nostalgic—there's nothing like Cleveland Stadium brown mustard, spicy and vinegary and worthy of leaving the ballpark. 440-461-2885; stadiummustard.com

4
VELLA FAMILY'S DRY MONTEREY JACK
The Vella family's Dry Monterey Jack, rubbed with unsweetened cocoa powder and black pepper and aged seven to ten months, makes an unforgettable grilled sandwich. 800-848-0505; vellacheese.com

5
WÜSTHOF CLASSIC EIGHT-INCH DELI KNIFE
Don't blow the easy part. The Wüsthof Classic eight-inch deli knife has an offset handle for leverage and knuckle room for neatly cutting through crusty bread. The blade serrations handle soft bread, salami, and cheese without tearing. 800-734-8511; shopfosters.com

6
NODINE'S SMOKED HAM
Nodine's smoked ham, glazed with ground cloves and brown sugar, is handily spiral cut to the bone so you can pull the slices apart in your sleep. 800-222-2059; nodinesmokehouse.com

7
KOEZE CREAM-NUT PEANUT BUTTER
All-natural Koeze Cream-Nut peanut butter is made in Michigan from roasted Virginia peanuts. Velvety and intense, it's the best in America. 800-555-3909; koeze.com

8
LOULOU'S GARDEN CORNICHONS
Crunchy cornichons, tart dill, and sweet bread-and-butter pickles from Loulou's Garden are packed in white-wine or apple-cider vinegar with fresh herbs. 415-613-8520; loulousgarden.com

9
CENTO OLIVE-OIL-PACKED ITALIAN TUNA
Cento olive-oil-packed Italian tuna is as rich and "meaty" as pricier imports, so skip the mayo and simply add a drop of balsamic vinegar along with a couple of capers and a handful of chopped parsley. Available in supermarkets.

1

2

3 Stadium Mustard

4 VELLA CHEESE CO. BEAR FLAG BRAND SONOMA, CA DRY MONTEREY JACK CHEESE

5 WÜSTHOF CLASSIC SOLINGEN GERMANY X50 Cr Mo V15 4123/20cm

6

7 CREAM-NUT Natural PEANUT BUTTER MANUFACTURED BY KOEZE COMPANY GRAND RAPIDS MI 49509 INGREDIENTS: VIRGINIA PEANUTS & SEA SALT Net. Wt. 17 oz. (1 lb. 1 oz.) 481g

8 LOULOU'S GARDEN Cornichons NET WT. 16 oz

9 CENTO SOLID PACK LIGHT TUNA IN PURE OLIVE OIL · SALT ADDED NET WT. 6 OZ (170g) TONNO

STEAK TACOS

with Guacamole, Salsa, and Lime Crema

Kerry Simon | Palms Place | Las Vegas

I DIDN'T LIVE ON the West Coast as a kid, but I grew up on Mexican food because my uncle, who was a coach in New Mexico, made us tacos and tamales and tortillas every summer when he came to visit. When I became a chef, I started reading about the more serious side of the cuisine. Then the great Patricia Quintana, known as the "Julia Child of Mexico," came to the Plaza in New York, where I was working, to collaborate on a menu with us. I toured Mexico with her, wandering from Oaxaca to Veracruz, just absorbing everything: the chaos in the markets, the shapes and colors of ingredients, the restaurants. But my favorite thing was the taco stands. Perfect simplicity. That's what attracted me. Don't let the long list of ingredients below throw you—this is simple street food, and there's very little actual "cooking" involved. Eat these things with your hands and some icy-cold Coronas served with limes.

SERVES 6 TO 8

DIFFICULTY:

SPICE MIXTURE

2 tsp chipotle chile powder

2 tbsp garlic powder

2 tbsp paprika

2 tbsp ground cumin

3 tsp coarse salt

TACOS

3½ lb skirt steak, cut against the grain into strips (a little smaller than your little finger)

twenty 4-inch flour tortillas

½ cup canola oil

- Combine the spice mixture ingredients and toss with the steak to coat. Set aside.

- Preheat the oven to 300°F. Warm the tortillas on a baking sheet.

- Heat 2 large sauté pans to medium-high. When the pans are hot, add half the oil to each pan followed by half the seasoned meat. Spread the meat out evenly and cook without turning while you lay out warm tortillas on a clean work area to get ready for assembly. Cook meat for about 3 minutes, then turn, and cook for another 3 minutes, stirring occasionally to achieve an even coloring. After 3 minutes, turn off the heat and allow the meat to sit in the pan, becoming just cool enough for you to handle.

TIP: Ask your butcher for organic skirt steak (a long, flat part of the chest muscle); it doesn't have any hormones, it marinates beautifully, it's more flavorful than many other cuts, and it holds up to the other ingredients in the taco.

GUACAMOLE

6 ripe Hass avocados

juice of 4 limes

4 plum tomatoes, finely diced (about 2 cups)

1 red onion, minced (about 1 cup)

1 bunch fresh cilantro, coarsely chopped

2 tsp coarse salt

- TO MAKE THE GUACAMOLE: Lightly crush the avocados with a fork until almost smooth but still a little chunky. Evenly mix in the lime juice, tomatoes, onion, cilantro, and salt; cover and refrigerate.

  TIP: To halve an avocado, insert the tip of a knife along the side until you hit the pit. Cut around the avocado lengthwise, slicing all the way around. Twist the two halves in opposite directions, and the avocado will open perfectly. Scoop out the pit and the flesh with a spoon.

SALSA

1 jalapeño chile

1 red onion, sliced ¼ inch thick

4 plum tomatoes

¼ cup canola oil

1 tsp coarse salt

½ bunch fresh cilantro, roughly chopped

juice of 3 limes

- TO MAKE THE SALSA: Rub the jalapeño, onion, and tomatoes with the oil and roast in large sauté pan over medium-high heat, turning frequently until lightly charred all over. Set aside to cool. (For a milder salsa, use only half the jalapeño.) When cooled, coarsely chop and process in a food processor with the salt, pulsing until almost smooth but still just a little chunky. Transfer to a bowl, add the cilantro and lime juice, cover, and refrigerate.

LIME CREMA

2 cups sour cream

juice of 2 limes

- TO MAKE THE LIME CREMA: Whisk the sour cream together with the lime juice.

CABBAGE

1 large head napa cabbage (Chinese cabbage), cut into thin strips

juice of 2 limes

CONTINUED FROM

- TO SERVE: Spread ½ tablespoon guacamole on each warmed tortilla. Follow this with a large pinch of cabbage that has been tossed with the juice of the limes. Distribute the meat evenly and fold the tortillas up end to end. Serve immediately on a large platter with the salsa, crema, guacamole, and a bag of your favorite tortilla chips.

  TIP: The salsa, crema, and guacamole can be prepared up to 2 hours ahead of time, wrapped tightly, and refrigerated. When wrapping the guacamole, press a layer of plastic wrap directly onto the surface (and/or keep avocado pits in the bowl) to avoid discoloration from oxidation.

A YEAR WITHOUT SANDWICHES

ONE WRITER PLEDGES TO FORGO THE JOY OF THE SANDWICH
TO LOSE A FEW POUNDS. THE SANDWICH WINS.

By Tom Chiarella

ONE YEAR, IN HOPES OF losing weight, I gave up bread. I waved it off at restaurants, didn't buy it. I ordered my burgers and egg salad like an old man: on a plate of lettuce, with a pickle, maybe.

I lost weight, but it wasn't worth it. You give up bread and you figure you'll miss toast, or the crust of a baguette, or pumpernickel seeds. But what you miss is sun-warm tomatoes between bread. Blood-red slices of roast beef. Paper-thin layers of white onions. Marmalade. The knife-curl of peanut butter. The weight of a tuna salad. None of these works particularly well on its own on a plate. They demand bread.

I figured it would be an easy enough year. I told myself I'd had enough sandwiches and that I'd be better off in the long run. There's always soup. I went into spring thinking, This isn't so bad. I might never have another sandwich again. Then one afternoon in early summer, I watched my girlfriend's daughter slice up a tomato, salt it lightly, and put it between two pieces of Roman Meal. Not long after, I saw a Reuben on the grill in a diner in Albany. Midsummer, I played poker at a game where the only food was a Dagwood, slice your own, on twenty-four inches of ciabatta. The whole night was a sandwich, noshed inch by inch by five four-flushers and a fish. I didn't eat a thing.

Late summer, I started ordering sandwiches and removing the bread. But that's just plain unattractive, and wasteful. So I started pushing the bread back with my teeth, acting as if I were eating the sandwich. That was comforting for a week or so. By October, I fell into ordering wraps, the lunchtime equivalent of sex with a condom.

Then, a year after I gave up bread, I found myself at the faux Carnegie Deli in the Mirage in Las Vegas. The guy next to me had one of those mountainous piles of lamp-hot pastrami stacked up like a ziggurat between two slices of rye. I looked at the waiter, then back to the sandwich, and up at the waiter's eyes again. I ordered that sandwich, bread toasted. I don't know why I expected him to chide me, but he didn't bat an eye. To him it was just another sandwich, another tick on the reliable second hand of the everyday. Then, I swear to God, I smiled. There at the end of my fast, I was reentering a part of the culture I had stupidly let myself forget, the one that pleasures itself in the sublime and pleasant swell of the hour we call lunch. Now, once again, I was ordering a sandwich, the most ruddy and reliable transaction I'll ever know.

White Bean and Italian Sausage

CHILI

David Bull | Congress | Austin

SERVES 4 TO 6

DIFFICULTY:

EASY | REASONABLE | WORTH THE EFFORT

1 tbsp canola oil

1 lb hot Italian fennel sausage links

1 tbsp olive oil

5 oz pancetta, diced

1 large yellow onion, diced

6 cloves garlic, minced

1 green bell pepper, seeded and diced

2 cups dried cannellini beans, rinsed

1 tbsp finely chopped fresh oregano leaves

2 tsp red pepper flakes

8 cups chicken stock

coarse salt and freshly ground black pepper

- Film a large stockpot with canola oil and place over medium-high heat. Brown the sausage on all sides. Reduce the heat to low and cook through, 8 to 10 minutes. Remove the sausage from the pan and let cool. Discard the grease.

- In the same pan, heat the olive oil and pancetta. Render the pancetta over low heat until crisp, 7 to 9 minutes. Add the onion and cook until soft and translucent, 5 to 6 minutes. Add the garlic and sauté until golden, about 3 minutes. Add the remaining ingredients, increase the heat, and bring to a boil. Dice the sausage and return to the chili mixture. Lower the heat and simmer until the beans are tender, at least 1½ hours, stirring occasionally. Season with salt and pepper to taste.

GARNISH

sour cream

½ cup scallions cut into long strips

½ cup Fried Leeks (recipe follows)

- Serve each bowl of chili with a dollop of sour cream and some scallions and fried leeks.

FRIED LEEKS

2 leeks (white parts only), cleaned and cut into fine threads

1 cup canola oil

coarse salt

- Bring a small saucepan of water to boil and blanch leek threads for 5 to 8 seconds. Drain and squeeze the excess moisture from the leeks, patting dry with paper towels. In a large skillet, heat the canola oil over high heat until almost smoking. Add the leeks and fry until they just start to turn golden brown. Drain on paper towels. Season with coarse salt to taste.

ESQUIRE
Classics

PRETTY EASY RECIPES FOR SOME OF THE BEST SOUPS OF ALL TIME.

Reprinted from the *Esquire Cookbook*, 1955

FRENCH ONION SOUP

From Pharamond, Paris.

Peel and slice 8 onions very thin. Poach gently until soft and clear in I stick sweet butter, seasoned with salt, hand-milled pepper, I teaspoon Dijon mustard, and 3 pinches of thyme or marjoram. Meanwhile, heat $1/4$ cup dry white wine with 4 cups chicken broth. Sprinkle the onions with a trifle of flour and work smooth, then add the broth mixture. Stir well. Put in individual marmites and flavor each serving with I teaspoon American apple brandy or French Calvados. Float on a $3/4$-inch-thick round of French bread, heaped with grated Parmesan cheese. Brown briefly under broiler. Delicious for 4.

ONION SOUP PROVENÇAL

For 4 to 6, peel and slice thin 4 large red onions. Heat 6 tablespoons butter or margarine in a heavy pot. Cook the onions in the butter until they're soft and golden. Add 3 cups of chicken stock, a dash of Maggi seasoning, and 2 cups of beer. Simmer, covered, for 45 minutes. Meanwhile, make 6 pieces of toast and sprinkle them generously with grated Parmesan cheese. Heat soup bowls in oven or in hot water. Preheat broiler. Season the soup with I teaspoon salt and $1/4$ teaspoon pepper. Pour into hot soup bowls, float a piece of cheese-toast on top of each, and pop under broiler for I minute.

ONION SOUP

A quicker version

Melt 2 tablespoons butter. Add 6 onions, sliced thin, and cook slowly until soft and tender but not brown. Add I quart consommé or beef stock and boil for 3 minutes. Season to taste. Pour into individual small casseroles, float toast on top, and add thin slice of Swiss cheese to the toast. Run the casseroles under the broiler until the cheese melts, then serve instantly. Serves 3 or 4.

VICHYSSOISE

From the Flamingo Hotel, Las Vegas

Chop up I cupful of the white part of leeks; chop I white onion fine. Melt 3 tablespoons butter in a heavy iron pot. Sauté the leeks and onion in the butter until they are soft but not brown. Meantime, mince raw, peeled potatoes until you have 2 cupfuls. When leeks are soft, sprinkle over them I tablespoon flour and stir in I quart strong chicken broth. Add the potatoes and cook gently until they fall apart; then strain the soup through a sieve so the soup will have a heavy consistency. Chill. Just before serving, slowly beat in I pint of heavy cream, I tablespoon salt, and a pinch of cayenne. Ladle into soup cups, top with finely chopped chives, and serve very cold. Serves 6 to 8.

MINESTRONE

From Little Venice Restaurant, New York

To 2 quarts of good strong beef stock, add the following diced vegetables: 4 stalks celery, I large carrot, I leek, with the top, 5 large leaves of cabbage, I large potato, and I $1/2$ cups canned kidney beans. Simmer for 30 minutes. Add 4 tablespoons elbow macaroni and simmer for 20 minutes longer. Season to taste. Serve piping hot, sprinkled with grated Parmesan cheese. Eat with chunks of Italian bread. Serves 6.

PETITE MARMITE

From the Blackstone Hotel, Chicago

Put I quart extra-rich chicken or beef stock in a marmite. Add diamond-cut pieces of carrot, chicken, beef, and tongue, plus slices of marrow and a sprinkling of chives. Let it bubble and blend on a very low flame until every item is tender. Long, slow cooking is the secret. Cook separately and add cooked fresh frozen peas at the last minute. Serve with two diamond-cut cheese croutons on each service plate. Serves 3 or 4.

CLAM CHOWDER

Originally published in Esquire's *November 1984 issue.*

WILLIAM STYRON grew up on the edge of the Chesapeake Bay—you can still hear southern Virginia in his voice—therefore William Styron grew up on clam chowder. Chowder, Styron assures us, isn't just a Yankee dish, as some people think. Some of the finest clams in America come from the bay. Indeed, he says, the cherrystone clam is named after a Chesapeake island. He may be a Yankee now, but he is not a man to forget his roots. For years he's served his clam chowder as the main course for brunch around Thanksgiving at his Vineyard Haven home or during Christmas in his old Roxbury, Connecticut, farmhouse. His recipe evolved over the years—it's one he grew up with and one to which he's added, as he puts it, "an interesting new wrinkle." That wrinkle is none other than the Cuisinart. He uses the julienne blade of his machine, transforming the potatoes into "thin silvers with wonderful texture and delicacy, as opposed to the traditional cubes or chunks." Styron's other secret in this tasty chowder: Don't peel the potatoes. The skins add taste, texture, and nutrients. And one final pointer: If you're William Styron and have been opening clams since practically before you could walk, you'll have no problem opening fresh—that is, live—clams. Otherwise, you may want to steam them open, which takes about ten minutes, or put the clams in the freezer for ten minutes until their muscles relax and they open their shells.

SERVES 6 TO 8

5 dozen cherrystone clams

3 or 4 slices bacon or a 2-inch cube of salt pork, diced

1 large onion, finely chopped

6 potatoes with skins

ground black pepper

3 cups milk, heated

- Open by hand or steam open the clams, saving the juice. (If steaming open, add 4 cups of water to a large pot and steam the clams, covered, for 10 minutes.)

- Cook the bacon or salt pork in a large kettle until crisp. Add the onion to the fat and cook until translucent, Run the potatoes through the Cuisinart with the julienne blade, then chop the strips into 2-inch lengths. (If a Cuisinart is not available, try slicing the potatoes into the thinnest possible matchsticks.)

- Chop the clams coarsely—don't use the Cuisinart, as you run the risk of turning them into puree—and add, along with the reserved clam juice, to the onion. Simmer the mixture for 5 minutes, then add the potatoes. Add pepper to taste. (No salt is needed.) Simmer for 20 minutes, pour in the heated milk, and simmer 5 minutes more. Serve piping hot.

LOBSTER BISQUE

For 6 people, here is an entire meal: Undercook 2 medium lobsters, crack shells, and remove the meat from shells and large claws, run meat through the fine blade of chopper. Break body and small claws, cover with water, and boil for 20 minutes. Strain. Add I quart milk to liquid and bring to boiling point. Melt 6 tablespoons butter, then stir in 2 tablespoons flour and 2 cups oyster crackers rolled to a dust. Gradually add this thickener to the hot milk and cook, stirring, for 5 minutes. Stir until thick and smooth, add the lobster meat, and season with salt and Tabasco sauce. Dust each serving with paprika.

CRAB GUMBO

From Harvey's Famous Restaurant, Washington, D.C.

For 4 big servings, chop I ½ onions and 2 green peppers, and crush I clove garlic. Sauté them in 3 ounces butter until soft. Add 2 quarts fish or clam broth and ½ cup washed rice; boil slowly for I5 minutes. Add I can okra, ½ can crab claw meat, 2 hard-shell crabs cut into 6 pieces each, 3 peeled and sliced tomatoes, ½ teaspoon sugar, and I tablespoon Worcestershire sauce. Cook slowly for 20 minutes. Add salt, thyme, and cayenne to taste. Sprinkle with chopped parsley and serve hot.

CHAPTER 3: DINNER

SUNDAY GRAVY

Peter McAndrews | Modo Mio | Philadelphia

BEING OF IRISH HERITAGE, and growing up in a household not quite culinarily diverse, I was often mystified by the food at the homes of my Italian-American friends in the neighborhood. There always seemed to be a party, and they took their food seriously. Sunday dinner was considered almost sacred. Fortunately for me, scoring an invitation was not hard, because most Italian families had an open-door policy. The fare was always referred to as pasta and gravy, with meats served separately after the pasta. As I learned to cook, I tried to replicate these mystical sauces, without much success. Then I married a second-generation Italian-American whose family brought this magnificent recipe over from the Old Country. Here's my version, best prepared as you drink a nice glass of red.

SERVES 8 TO 10

DIFFICULTY:

about ½ cup olive oil

3 lb sweet or hot Italian sausage (or mixture), cut into 3-inch slices

2 lb your favorite meatballs (about 24 formed meatballs)

3 lb country-style pork ribs (see **Tip**), preferably on the bone

2 lb pork neck bones (though any beef or pork bones will do)

2 Spanish or other mild onions, finely chopped

8 cloves garlic, minced

one 12-oz can tomato paste

five 28-oz cans whole peeled tomatoes (preferably San Marzano) with juices, crushed by hand until no whole tomatoes remain

3 bay leaves

hefty pinch of sugar

coarse salt to taste (2 to 3 tsp)

cooked pasta for serving

- Coat the cooking surface of large heavy-bottomed stockpot (at least 12 quarts—we're talking about a huge pot) with some of the olive oil, place over medium-low heat, and brown all the meats on all sides, working one at a time in this order: sausage, and remove; meatballs, and remove; ribs, and remove; then pork bones, leaving these in the pot. (Add more olive oil as needed.)

- Add the onions to the pork bones and slowly brown, stirring occasionally, 3 to 5 minutes. Add the garlic and lightly brown, stirring occasionally, 3 to 5 minutes. Add the tomato paste and stir to coat onions and pork bones. Slowly cook until the paste begins to thicken and turn deep reddish brown, about 5 minutes. Add the tomatoes, bay leaves, and sugar. Stir well, making sure you get down to the bottom, and bring

to a low boil. Lower the heat and simmer uncovered until the sauce begins to thicken.

- After 1 hour, add the ribs; after another hour, add the sausage; at 3 hours, add the meatballs. Continue to simmer until a layer of oil forms on the top, about another hour. Season to taste with salt. Use a slotted spoon to transfer the meat to a serving platter. Ladle the sauce over your favorite pasta and serve.

TIP: Sold as slabs or individually, country-style ribs are a meatier cut from the rib or sirloin end of the pork loin.

BARBEQUE-SPICE-RUBBED SKIRT STEAK

with Charred Onions and Jalapeños

Dave Walzog | SW Steakhouse | Las Vegas

SERVES 4

DIFFICULTY:

SPICE RUB

2 tbsp chili powder

2 tsp garlic powder

1 tbsp onion powder

1 tsp Spanish smoked paprika (La Chinata is the best)

2 tbsp light brown sugar

2 tsp coarse salt

1 tsp dried oregano

STEAKS

2 tbsp balsamic vinegar

2 tbsp cider vinegar

2 tbsp corn oil

½ cup ketchup

two 16-oz skirt steaks

corn oil for searing

Charred Onions and Jalapeños (recipe follows)

- TO MAKE THE SPICE RUB: Combine all the ingredients in a small bowl.

- TO MAKE STEAKS: Combine the balsamic vinegar, cider vinegar, corn oil, and ketchup in a bowl. Add the skirt steaks and marinate for 2 hours.

- Meanwhile, preheat the oven to 375°F. Remove the steaks, blot the excess marinade with a paper towel, and rub both sides with the spice rub. Heat a 12-inch cast-iron skillet over medium-high heat until just smoking. Generously film the bottom with corn oil to prevent the spices from burning. Cut the steaks in half so they fit in the pan. Working with two pieces at a time, sear the steaks for 3 minutes on each side, transferring them to a baking sheet when each batch is done. Place the pan in the oven and cook until the internal temperature is 115° to 125°F, about 6 minutes. Remove from the oven and let rest for 3 to 4 minutes before slicing.

- Serve the steaks topped with the charred onions and jalapeños.

CHARRED ONIONS AND JALAPEÑOS

2 white onions, peeled and cut into 1-inch slices

6 jalapeño chiles

4 small bell peppers (mixed red and yellow, if possible)

corn oil (just enough to coat vegetables)

coarse salt and freshly ground black pepper

1½ tbsp unsalted butter

1 cup chicken stock

2 sprigs fresh thyme

- TO MAKE THE CHARRED ONIONS AND JALAPEÑOS: Lay the vegetables on a baking sheet, coat with corn oil, and season with salt and pepper.

- Heat a 12-inch cast-iron skillet over medium-high heat until just smoking. Working in small batches, char the vegetables on all sides. (Alternatively, the vegetables can be charred on a grill.) Return all the vegetables to the pan, then add the butter, stock, and thyme and cook uncovered over medium heat until the vegetables are fork-tender and the stock is reduced to a thickened sauce, about 20 minutes.

FILET MIGNON
au Poivre

Bill Rodgers | Keens Steakhouse | New York City

SERVES 2

DIFFICULTY:

1½ tbsp whole black peppercorns

two 8-oz filet mignon steaks, about 2 inches thick

coarse salt

1 tbsp unsalted butter

1 tbsp canola oil

2 tbsp minced shallot

3½ tbsp brandy

3 tbsp demi-glace* (see Note)

¾ cup heavy cream

- In a pepper grinder on the loosest setting, crack the peppercorns. (You want chunks, not dust.) Dredge both sides of the steaks in the peppercorns and season with salt.

- In a cast-iron pan, melt the butter with the oil over medium heat. When the butter stops sizzling, add the steaks. Cook until the internal temperature is 115° to 125°F, about 4 minutes on each side. Remove the steaks and cover with foil.

- Pour out most of any remaining fat and return the pan to heat. Add the shallot and scrape up the bits of meat and pepper from the bottom of the pan. After 10 seconds, pull the pan from the heat and slowly add 3 tablespoons brandy, keeping your face away from the pan—the brandy fumes can ignite. Return the pan to the heat and tilt it toward the burner until the brandy ignites. Stir and scrape again. Reduce the brandy until it's syrupy, add the demi-glace, and cook for 30 seconds more. Add the cream and continue to cook, constantly whisking, 3 to 5 minutes. Add a touch of salt and the remaining ½ tablespoon brandy. Serve the steaks with the sauce poured over them.

    NOTE: Demi-glace is a concentrated brown-sauce reduction. It is available at Whole Foods and other specialty-foods markets.

We tried this recipe once without the demi-glace. Still tasty, but use it if at all possible.

BEEFSTEAK

Florentine

Andrew Carmellini | Locanda Verde | New York City

IT WOULD BE DIFFICULT to come up with a better illustration of true Tuscan cooking than beefsteak Florentine. One of the classics—it has its own Facebook page—it's traditionally made on a wood-fired grill with the region's Chianina beef, one of the oldest breeds in existence. To accommodate urbanites who don't have a grill, my version calls for hot pan-searing and an oven finish. The porterhouse cut gives you meat from both sides of the rib: the strip and the soft tenderloin, protected by the edge of the bone. The puree has a touch of honey to offset any bitterness in the garlic, but don't think of this as a honey-glazed steak. The puree disappears into the meat. In true Tuscan style, you don't even know it's there.

SERVES 2

DIFFICULTY:

EASY	REASONABLE	WORTH THE EFFORT

ROASTED-GARLIC PUREE

2 heads garlic, tops sliced off to expose cloves

3 tbsp extra-virgin olive oil

1 tbsp sherry vinegar

1 tsp honey

¼ tsp freshly ground black pepper

½ tsp coarse salt

STEAK

canola oil for searing

one 23- to 30-oz porterhouse steak (about 2½ inches thick)

coarse salt and freshly ground black pepper

- TO MAKE THE ROASTED-GARLIC PUREE: Preheat the oven to 450°F. Place each head of garlic in the center of a square of aluminum foil, drizzle each with 1 tablespoon olive oil, and seal the foil to make an airtight packet. Place the packets in a shallow baking dish in the oven and roast until the garlic cloves are soft, about 1 hour. Unseal the packets.

- When the garlic is cool enough to handle, turn each head upside down over a small bowl and squeeze out the soft cloves. Add the remaining ingredients and the remaining 1 tablespoon oil and whisk to a paste.

- TO MAKE THE STEAK: Preheat the oven to 450°F. Place a large cast-iron skillet over medium-high heat until hot. (The pan should stop just short of smoking.) Lightly film the skillet with oil and add the steak, generously seasoned with salt and pepper. Sear the meat on each side for 2½ to 3 minutes. Because this steak is so thick, use tongs to rotate the meat, lightly searing the edges. Transfer the steak to a baking sheet and place in the oven. Cook for 8 minutes, then flip and cook for another 8 minutes for medium-rare (internal temperature 115° to 125°F).

- Remove the pan from the oven and let the meat rest for at least 15 minutes (internal temperature rises to 120° to 130°F) before slathering with roasted-garlic puree. Return the pan to the oven to heat the steak, about 3 minutes. Using a knife with a thin, sharp blade, carve the meat away from the bone into thick slices.

STEAK INFORMATION CENTER

By Francine Maroukian

A man should know his meat. We can help. We tell you everything you need to know on steak types, grades, and cooking times.

WHY BEEF IS AGED, AND HOW

Beef must be aged to allow natural enzymes to break down the fibrous connective tissue that holds the muscle together. There are two ways to age beef:

Dry aging: Expensive and time consuming. The beef is stored in temperature- and humidity-controlled coolers for up to six weeks. Moisture evaporates, improving texture and concentrating flavor. Between the evaporation and trimming of the thin coating of mold that develops, there's weight loss of up to 20 percent.

Wet aging: The beef is refrigerated in vacuum-sealed plastic and allowed to tenderize in its own juices. No evaporation means no moisture is lost. Less waste but also less concentrated taste.

SOME TYPES OF BEEF YOU SHOULD KNOW ABOUT

Heritage: From rare heirloom breeds, pasture-raised on small farms without the hormones or pesticides used in conventional agribusiness.

Rare "red" cattle (the same breed that produces Kobe beef)*:* Raised in Texas by HeartBrand Beef—the only herd outside of Japan. They started with eleven head of cattle, which were guarded by armed Texas Rangers for fourteen years while the herd grew to more than five thousand. (heartbrandbeef.com)

Angus: Aberdeen-Angus is a pure breed found in the United States, England, Scotland, and Ireland. Certified Angus Brand is a brand name and may or may not include meat from Aberdeen-Angus.

Grass-fed: Healthier but, some say, less flavorful than corn-fed. Raised in open pastures. Not necessarily organic. (Grain-finished cattle—which are switched from grass to grain for the last few weeks before slaughter—develop more marbling.)

THE GRADES OF MEAT

Prime: What you want. Typically found only at fine butcher shops, its interlacing of intramuscular fat—like a cobweb—ensures tenderness, juiciness, and flavor.

Choice: Pretty good. More affordable and accessible than prime; moderate marbling still yields juicy, flavorful cuts.

Select: You're on a plane.

GENERALLY IMPORTANT POINT (Cooking)
Cooking times in recipes are predicated on starting with meat that's not too cold. All steaks should be taken out of the refrigerator at least thirty minutes before cooking.

THE PAN

☑ Lodge 10¼- and 12-inch cast-iron pan (see page 10).

☑ The pan must be hot enough to sear the meat on contact, to prevent surface moisture from creating steam, which can prevent browning.

☑ While some chefs say the pan should be "smoking" before adding oil, most call for the intuitive "hot but not smoking." Basically, really goddamn hot.

A NOTE ON SALT

☑ When you salt meat before cooking, you need a lot—and a lot falls off—so standard kosher salt will do. After cooking is the time to use good sea salt. It's pricey, but the large, crackly flakes are intense, so you don't need much.

HOW TO USE OIL

☑ Before the meat goes in, the skillet should be filmed with oil—it should coat the surface without pooling. (You can add it when the pan is cold or hot.) At the right temperature, the oil will shimmer and gently ripple, as if you dropped a pebble into a pond. It shouldn't spatter or smoke.

THE FINISH

☑ Meat's temperature keeps rising after cooking. Remove steaks from the heat when a meat thermometer reads 115° to 125°F. Then wait. During the all-important resting period, the temperature will rise to the medium-rare range, 120° to 130°F.

☑ Get a good thermometer, preferably with a digital probe and large readout, like the super-fast Thermapen (see page 11). It is a potentially life-changing device. (thermoworks.com)

☑ Always start with a recipe's minimum cooking time. You can't uncook a steak.

☑ If you don't have a thermometer and you don't want to cut into the meat, press the cartilage at the tip of your nose. That's what medium-rare feels like.

Butter-Poached
BONE-IN TOP LOIN

Michael Mina | Nobhill Tavern | Las Vegas

SERVES 2

DIFFICULTY:

EASY
REASONABLE
WORTH THE EFFORT

about 4½ cups Clarified Butter (recipe follows)

8 sprigs fresh thyme

3 shallots, coarsely chopped

a few garlic cloves, crushed

two 16- to 20-oz bone-in top loin steaks, 1¼ to 1½ inches thick

coarse salt and freshly ground black pepper

- In the top of a makeshift double boiler (a deep skillet just large enough to hold the steaks, sitting on top of a stockpot of simmering water), bring the clarified butter to between 140° and 150°F, using the probe of an instant-read meat thermometer to measure the temperature. To stabilize the temperature, keep the water at a gentle simmer, and regularly check the butter's temperature with the meat thermometer. (Don't let the probe touch the bottom of the pan—that will give you a false reading.)

- Add the thyme, shallots, and garlic. Season the steaks generously with salt and pepper and add them to the butter. For every inch of thickness, poach the meat for 30 minutes (the internal temperature should be 115° to 125°F). (If the butter doesn't totally cover the steaks, flip the steaks halfway through poaching.)

- Remove the steaks, letting the excess butter drip off. Reseason the steaks with salt and pepper and transfer to a very hot cast-iron pan or hot grill. Sear on each side to develop a brown crust, about 2 minutes total. Serve immediately.

CLARIFIED BUTTER

1 lb unsalted butter, cut into small pieces

- In a heavy-bottomed stockpot over very low heat, melt the butter. The milk solids will rise to the top as foam. The water in the butter will settle to the bottom. In the middle will be what you want: the fat. When all the butter is melted, skim and discard the foam and use a ladle to transfer the butter fat—the very yellow liquid—to a clean container. (When the liquid you're ladling out starts becoming much lighter in color, you're done.) Discard the water.

See page 189 for Truffled Macaroni and Cheese recipe.

STEAK NIGHT

By Scott Raab

I GREW UP BARELY MIDDLE CLASS. Before the divorce, my dad was a depressive salesman, and my mom was a homemaker; afterward, my father lived three thousand miles away, my mother was a receptionist, and we moved in with her parents—a retired railroad laborer and a bakery clerk. Millions of people believe in an alchemical bond between Jews and money; we had one toilet for four adults—while my great-grandmother was still alive—and three kids, an old Maxwell House can at the foot of the stairs for the boys to piss into, and no knowledge of even one protocol of the Elders of Zion.

Yet we ate like Rothschilds. The bakery and the appetizer merchant and the huckster—that's what Gram called the wop who peddled fruit and vegetables from his step van—covered most of the basics, and Katz, the kosher butcher, took care of our veal, poultry, and beef. Lavishly. Looking back, I don't know if Katz was shtupping Gram, or merely wished to, but I can think of no other explanation for the kind and quantity of stuff she toted home—especially his rib steaks, fresh, marbled slabs the likes of which mine eyes had never seen.

I see them again now, each week—rib or rib eyes from Whole Foods or a kosher shop in West Orange, New Jersey—on Steak Night. Two thick beauties—three pounds, give or take—salt, garlic, and a broiler pan dripping with grease and joy. It's no particular night, nor was it ever a conscious choice to nourish and share the best family values I knew—pink meat, sharp knives, and fat-laced, blood-drenched protein.

It's the best night of the week, always. Just ask the dog, who lies against my foot as we eat, yearning for the scraps to come. Better yet, ask my young son, raised like his old man: on steak.

"How's the beef?" I say.

"It's *great*," he says.

And in that moment, he and I are one. He's eating like a man, while I'm a boy once more.

STEAK

with Potatoes

Tom Colicchio | Craftsteak | New York City

MY PHILOSOPHY is to keep preparations simple, allowing the ingredients to shine. This dish started as a one-pot meal at Craftsteak, but I often find myself making it at home. It just requires a beautiful piece of hanger steak—named because it hangs down between the tenderloin and rib without being connected to a bone. There's only one, which is why many butchers save this cut for their own family. The addition of red onions, bacon, and vinegar hits the classic combination of sweet, salty, and acidic. I cut the steak into $3/4$-inch pieces, slicing against the grain. Anything less and the meat will lose its toothsome appeal.

SERVES 2

DIFFICULTY:

EASY | REASONABLE | WORTH THE EFFORT

1 lb hanger steak

coarse salt and freshly ground black pepper

1 tbsp canola oil

3 tbsp unsalted butter

6 sprigs fresh thyme

4 oz thickly sliced smoked bacon (4 slices), diced

10 oz fingerling potatoes, halved lengthwise if small, cut into $1/2$-inch rounds if larger

1 red onion, thinly sliced

1 clove garlic, minced

5 tbsp balsamic vinegar

- Place a 10-inch cast-iron skillet over high heat. Season the steak with salt and pepper. Add the oil to very hot skillet, and when it is almost smoking (the surface will start to shimmer), sear the meat for 4 minutes on each side. Reduce the heat to medium-low (letting the pan cool down a bit) and add butter and 3 sprigs of thyme. (The pan must cool down before you add the butter, or it will sizzle and burn on contact.) Using a spoon, baste the steak with butter for 2 to 3 minutes, flipping it once halfway through to cook it evenly. (The temperature for a medium-rare steak is about 135°F.) Remove the meat from the skillet and set aside.

- Discard all fat and thyme from skillet. Wipe clean with a paper towel. Over medium heat, cook the bacon to render the fat and slightly crisp the meat, about 5 minutes. Nestle in the potatoes (cut-side down if using halved potatoes) and cook until crisp and golden, 4 to 5 minutes. Turn the potatoes and continue cooking until tender, another 4 to 5 minutes. Add the onion and remaining thyme and cook, stirring occasionally, until the onion caramelizes and the potatoes are cooked through, 10 to 15 minutes. Lower the heat and add the garlic, and when you can smell its aroma, add the balsamic vinegar and cook to reduce, about 3 minutes.

- Carve the steak into ¾-inch slices and return to the skillet, arranging it atop the vegetables.

PEPPER-CRUSTED STRIP STEAKS

Charlie Palmer | Aureole | New York City

LIKE MANY CHEFS, I started my professional cooking life under the French influence. When I opened my first restaurant, Aureole, it was the early '80s and I did all of the early-'80s things, from splattering sauce on a plate to building a dessert that stood sixteen inches high. But at the end of the day, I'm really just a big American guy with a big American appetite—the kind of appetite it often takes a big slab of meat to satisfy. We've come full circle in this country when it comes to meat; small producers are determined to give us cleaner, more fully flavored beef, and many supermarkets are reopening their butcher counters so you don't have to buy some dinky precut steak that's been sitting in Cryovac. My philosophy is that if you're going to eat a steak, then eat a steak. Find a good butcher—no, wait, do more than find one, befriend one—and ask for a couple of big, well-marbled strips (cut from the boneless top loin, the equivalent of a porterhouse steak minus tenderloin and bone). Invest in some quality black peppercorns—so pungent you can smell them as soon as you open the package—and while you're at it, buy a small marble mortar and pestle. This is the most basic tool you can have in your kitchen. It's cheap, less than $25, and once you pulverize some hard spices in it—really crush them down and let their aroma waft up and hit you in the nose—you'll never buy pre-ground again. Get some crackly sea salt that you have to crush between your fingers and just let it rain down on your steak. This is as naked as a meal gets—there's nowhere to hide. It all comes down to the quality of the meat. So ask for steaks from the loin end of the strip (where the "eye" is bigger), and purchase by thickness rather than weight, as strip loins can vary in size. When cut from a big loin, 12 ounces may be the right weight, but the steak can be too thin to cook a nice mid-rare and still get a good seared crust. My advice: Just get a big-ass steak and deal with the leftovers later.

SERVES 2 HEARTILY

DIFFICULTY:

two 12- to 14-oz strip
steaks, about 1½ inch-
es thick (sometimes
sold as Delmonico, New
York, Kansas City, shell,
or sirloin club steak)

sea salt

½ cup whole black
peppercorns, coarsely
cracked (see Note)

grapeseed or
canola oil

2 tbsp unsalted butter

3 cloves garlic,
smashed

leaves from 4 sprigs
fresh thyme, chopped

- Preheat the oven to 350°F. Heat a heavy, ovenproof sauté pan over high heat.

- Meanwhile, salt the meat all over and press one side of each steak into cracked peppercorns. Film the bottom of the pan with oil and heat until almost smoking. (When it's hot enough, the oil will "roll" in the pan—sort of move on its own in little waves.) Immediately put the steaks in the pan, pepper-side down. For steaks on the rare side of medium-rare, sear until a crust forms, about 3 minutes on each side. Transfer to the oven for another 4 to 6 minutes. (This depends on the shape of the steak, but the target temperature for medium-rare is 130°F.)

- Remove the pan from the oven, and add the butter, garlic, and thyme. No further heat is needed; the hot pan will melt the butter. Baste the steaks. Let the steaks rest on a warmed plate until you can touch them without burning your fingertips.

NOTE: Grind the peppercorns with a mortar and pestle (texture: like Grape-Nuts cereal). It can take a while, but it's the only way to go.

TIP: Resting "evens out" the cooking. Also, if meat doesn't rest, juices bleed as it is sliced. For steaks this size, about 5 minutes should work. Better to rest too long and reheat than not to rest at all. If the steaks have gone too cold for your taste, zap under the broiler just to give them a little surface temperature.

THE PERFECT PRE-STEAK DRINK:
THE MARTINI

By David Wondrich

NOW, OUR FEELINGS FOR BROILED porterhouse are strong and deeply rooted, and we yield to no man, woman, child, or talking dog in our love for and appreciation of a dry gin martini. But to drink a martini with your steak is to do violence to both. The beef is far too bold for something as elegant as a properly balanced martini, while the martini's icy power renders the palate insensible to the steak's subtle gradations of flavor. No, with steak you drink wine or ale. But that doesn't mean you should forget about the cocktail. To the contrary: As misguided as it is to use the noble martini to lubricate your steak, it's equally wrong to have that steak without having a martini first. To properly enjoy the meat, you need every one of your pleasure receptors in good working order, loose, clean, and ready. No drink gets them that way more efficiently than the martini. No other cocktail—no other beverage—delivers the cold, tangy flavors that, for some reason, enhance the meat experience. If the steak is Christ, the martini is its John the Baptist, preparing a suffering and hopeless humanity for the good news that is to come.

YOUR FIRST STEAK:
THE SALISBURY DINNER

By Ross McCammon

LET'S GET THIS OUT OF THE WAY RIGHT now: The Salisbury steak in the Stouffer's Salisbury-steak frozen dinner is awful. It tastes like a giant stale crouton that's been soaked in beef broth for a few minutes, then injected with gelatin, then glazed with the juice of sautéed raisins. It has the mouthfeel of raw sausage. Which is not at all surprising. The surprising part is that although it tastes horrible, eating one twenty-five years after you last ate one is not a horrible experience. It's a rich, satisfying experience. Because the Salisbury steak is the first steak a man ever eats. It's the foundation steak—even if it's minced beef that is only supposed to resemble steak. It represents the world of anachronistic yet still accessible "first foods." For me, it tastes like 1978 through 1982, which were brown, sort of caramel-ized years anyway. When you bite down on a light, beefy morsel, the fat of your childhood oozes out. According to the box, what also oozes out is tomato paste, soy-sauce powder, autolyzed yeast extract, and water. But all those things (plus lactic acid and rolled oats) add up to the food equivalent of playing Galaga. Somehow, it's wonderful. The same experience could be had with Gorton's fish sticks. Or Campbell's SpaghettiOs. Because these are our first foods. And the Salisbury is our first steak, the steak that goes before—the prophet, the pioneer. Whether or not it's good isn't important. How it makes you feel is the important part. And how the Stouffer's Salisbury steak makes you feel is hopeful that there's something out there that tastes pretty much like this, only way, way better. And there is.

Braised Beef
SHORT RIBS

John Besh | Restaurant August | New Orleans

I GREW UP ON THE BAYOU AND never strayed far because New Orleans has always been, and still is, a hell of a place to cook. Food has more cultural significance here. No matter where in the world early settlers came from—Italy, Spain, Senegal, Haiti—and whether free or enslaved, they assimilated into the Creole culture, embracing everything from language to cooking. That's why dishes like gumbo and jambalaya have so many ingredients—every culture stirred a bit into the pot. I try to deliver some of that complexity in this one-pot meal while keeping the ingredient list short by using a reduction of naturally spicy Zinfandel with a touch of sugar, a combo that adds backbone and works wonders with the fattiness of the meat. There was a time when you couldn't give short ribs away in American restaurants. It was fillet of beef this and lobster that. But as we've grown more comfortable—culinarily speaking—we've begun to identify with peasant-style cooking, the kind of food our grandparents might have made. This is one of those dishes. The ribs come from the chuck section, where the meat contains a lot of connective tissue and needs slow, moist cooking.

SERVES 4

DIFFICULTY:

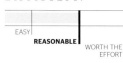

EASY | REASONABLE | WORTH THE EFFORT

4 lb beef short ribs (see Tip)

coarse salt and freshly ground black pepper

3 cups Zinfandel

1/2 cup sugar

3/4 cup canned diced tomatoes

2 cups beef broth

1 tbsp minced garlic

leaves from 3 sprigs fresh thyme

2 bay leaves

6 tbsp canola oil

1 large onion, diced (2 cups)

2 carrots, diced (1/2 cup)

2 stalks celery, diced (1/2 cup)

2 oz dried mushrooms, preferably porcini

- Season the short ribs with salt and pepper; be rather generous. In a mixing bowl, whisk together the Zinfandel, sugar, tomatoes, beef broth, garlic, thyme, bay leaves, and a pinch of salt.

- Pour the canola oil into a heavy pot or Dutch oven (at least 5 quarts) and place over high heat. When the oil is hot, working in small batches, brown the meat. Turn each piece to brown on all sides before removing from the pot. (A sturdy pot that conducts heat well has a lot to do with the success of this dish. Get yourself a cast-iron pot. It'll outlast you.) When all the beef is browned and removed from the pot, add the

onion, carrots, and celery, allowing the onion to cook until browned, about 10 minutes, stirring frequently. Return the beef to the pot along with the wine mixture. Allow the wine mixture to come to a boil before reducing heat, skimming fat from the surface. After simmering for several minutes, add the mushrooms. Cover and simmer over very low heat until meat is fork tender and nearly falling off the bone, $1\frac{1}{2}$ to 2 hours.

- Once the beef has cooked, remove from the pot and keep warm. Turn up the heat and reduce the pot liquid until thickened, about 10 minutes. Season with salt and pepper to taste. Transfer the ribs to four shallow bowls, spooning the liquid over the top.

TIP: Ribs cut flanken style (across the bone) are easier to deal with than those cut English style (parallel to the bone), but are slightly more fatty.

THINGS A MAN SHOULD KNOW ABOUT
GRILLING

By John Mariani

Charcoal or gas? Gas or charcoal? Charcoal probably gives your food a better flavor. But gas . . . it's just so easy.

Still, charcoal grills aren't that hard to get going. Have a drink. It'll be ready soon.

You can grill just about anything over direct heat—right above the coals or the flame—but sometimes, indirect grilling is better. Big cuts of meat, entire chickens, anything dripping with fat—for these, shove all the coals to one side of the charcoal grill and use the opposite side, or, on a gas grill, use less flame and don't cook the food directly over it.

A covered grill is a hotter grill.

Food cooked in a covered grill tastes smokier. This is usually a good thing, but not always. Also, it's easier to overcook food when the grill is covered. Why? Because you can't see the food.

"Barbecuing" usually refers to cooking big things like pork butt, beef brisket, and whole hogs over low heat for a long time. Grilling hamburgers is not barbecuing. That's grilling.

A good way to oil your grill's grid before using: Chop an onion in half, dip the cut side in vegetable oil, and rub it all over the grid.

The resealable plastic bag was made for marinating.

Basting meat with leftover marinade during cooking is a good idea. Using leftover marinade as a finishing sauce is not. Because of the raw-meat juice, of course.

To clean your grill grate, use a little soapy water at the beginning of the season. Then hit it with a wire brush, when it's still warm, after each use. That's it.

A pot holder is not the same thing as a grilling mitt. Pot holders are for ovens.

To test food for doneness, a cake tester or metal skewer can make you look like a genius. Stick it into the middle of whatever meat you're grilling, then hold it to your chin. If it's cool, keep cooking. If it's warm, you're at medium-rare. If it's pretty hot, yank the food off the grill.

Careful with tongs. Squeeze too tight and you squeeze the juice out. Same goes for maneuvering using a fork or knife.

Spatulas.

On gadgetry: Baskets, toppers, rib racks, vegetable holders, drip pans—all good tools, though not all essential. Only buy what you'll use.

A cool gadget for charcoal grills: the electric charcoal igniter. You plug it in, set it in the grill, top it with charcoal, and within about eight minutes the coals will be on their way to readiness. No lighter fluid needed.

But nothing beats the chimney starter.

Charcoal is ready when 80 percent of the coals are ash-gray.

If the fire gets too weak (you can hold your hand just above the grill for four or five seconds), try pushing the coals closer together. If it's too hot (two seconds, max), spread the coals out and move your food to the edge. If the coals start to burn down and disappear, add more—but remember, that brings the temperature down too.

You can put barbecue sauce on just about anything. But only do so in the last ten or fifteen minutes of cooking—the sugar in the sauce can char.

Add just about anything to mayonnaise for a sauce or a spread. Hot sauce, lemon zest, basil, mustard, whatever. Hard not to make it taste good.

An interesting steak sauce: Dijon mustard, melted butter, Worcestershire.

The basic marinade: an oil (olive, canola, grapeseed, etc.), an acid (vinegar, lemon juice, yogurt, wine, etc.), herbs, and spices. Experiment. And a smashed garlic clove never hurts.

If you forgot to make a marinade—food has to sit in the marinade for a few hours to, you know, marinate—make a rub real fast. About a half-hour before grilling (or even at the last second), massage it into the meat. Use what you like—pepper, cinnamon, dried herbs, cayenne, chili powder, brown sugar, cumin, paprika . . .

Always salt beef a good half-hour before grilling. You're not flavoring. You're tenderizing, and tenderizing takes time.

Don't overmix or manhandle your burgers. You want them just barely formed into a patty. Otherwise, the meat will get tough.

And please don't press the burgers down with a spatula as they cook. Unless you like a dry hamburger.

When to add the cheese: After flipping (obviously), a minute or two before the second side is done. Then close the cover.

To grill fresh sausage: First, precook it by poking it with a fork and simmering it in water until just about cooked, ten minutes tops. Then grill it till it's browned and a little bubbly, probably five minutes.

The kebab was a wonderful invention. It's like a whole meal on a stick.

A kebab secret: If you want the meat medium-rare, pack it tight on the skewer. For medium-well, space the pieces out.

Don't forget that skewers get hot.

One inch is the best thickness for a steak (including fish steaks) or pork chop. It's the easiest to get right—a nice exterior crust, a juicy middle.

That goes for lamb chops, too. And there is nothing like a grilled lamb chop. A little olive oil, salt, and pepper, and throw it on over high heat.

Chicken is tricky. It dries out, it burns, it's susceptible to slight differences in grill temperature. If you have a bunch of chicken pieces on the grill, flip them frequently and move them around the grill a lot according to which pieces are cooking fastest and where the grill is the hottest.

Don't forget about vegetables. Toss some thin asparagus with olive oil, salt, and pepper, throw it on, and it'll be done before you can go grab another beer. Delicious.

Wrap small vegetables in a foil packet and rest it over high heat. Poke a few holes in the foil to let the smoky flavor in.

There is no fruit you can't grill (I don't think). Pineapples, bananas, cantaloupe, oranges, peaches—slice or cut in half, brush with melted butter and, if you want, brown sugar, and grill. There are few tastier desserts than grilled fruit, and somehow, it always surprises people.

John Mariani is *Esquire*'s food and drinks correspondent and the coauthor of *Grilling for Dummies*.

BRAISED BEEF BRISKET

with Horseradish Cream and Pickled Onion

Suzanne Goin | Lucques | Los Angeles

I GREW UP COOKING for my dad and trying desperately to please him. He had a sophisticated palate, but unexpected, unfussy things seemed to make him happiest. There's something inherently comforting and reassuring about brisket—it has an Old World vibe. Searing a piece of meat this large may take longer and be messier than you imagined, but the secret to a great braise is getting a good sear at the beginning and the end. You want the succulent, tender texture of the meat to have the contrast of a crisp, caramelized exterior—otherwise it just tastes like stewed meat. Good news is, you can do the messy work in advance—even the day before—and reheat the brisket right before serving.

SERVES 6

DIFFICULTY:

1 large flat or first-cut beef brisket, 5½ to 6 lb with ½-inch fat cap (see Tip)

2 tbsp coarse salt

3 tbsp fresh thyme leaves

2 bay leaves, crumbled

10 cloves garlic, peeled and smashed

3 dried chiles de árbol (broken in half), or 2 tsp red pepper flakes, crushed

1½ tbsp cracked black pepper

4 tbsp olive oil

2 onions, coarsely chopped

3 carrots, coarsely chopped

¼ cup balsamic vinegar

3 cups dark beer, such as Guinness or Samuel Smith

4 cups beef stock

Horseradish Cream (recipe follows)

Pickled Onion (recipe follows)

- Remove the brisket from the refrigerator 2 hours before cooking and season with the salt, thyme, bay leaves, garlic, chiles, and black pepper.

- Preheat the oven to 325°F. Place a large, heavy roasting pan (preferably with a lid) over two burners at high heat for 2 minutes. Add 3 tablespoons of the olive oil and wait a minute. Place the seasoned brisket, fat-side down, in the pan and sear on both sides until deep brown, about 8 minutes a side. Once both sides are well browned, remove the brisket and reduce the heat to medium-high. Add the remaining 1 tablespoon olive oil and the vegetables to the pan and cook until caramelized, 8 to 10 minutes. Stir often with a wooden spoon, scraping up all the crusty bits. Turn off the heat (so the liquids won't evaporate immediately), add the vinegar, then the beer. Turn the heat

CONTINUED

back up to medium-high and cook to reduce the beer by one-fourth. Add the beef stock and bring to a boil over high heat. Return the brisket to the pan, settling it in so the vegetables surround the meat. (The stock should come just to the top of brisket. Add more stock if necessary.) Cover the pan tightly (with foil, if necessary) and braise in the oven for about 4 hours. If a fork slides in easily, the brisket is done. If the meat resists, cook another 15 minutes or so, being careful not to let it dry out. Turn up the oven temperature to 400°F.

- Carefully transfer the brisket to a baking sheet and return to the oven until the top is crisp, about 20 minutes. Strain the braising juices into a saucepan and skim off the fat. Let the meat rest for 10 minutes after it comes out of the oven. Place on a cutting board and slice thinly against the grain. Plate the meat, spoon the braising juices over it, and dollop with horseradish cream. Top with pickled onion and serve. Recommended side: mashed potatoes.

TIP: Look for meat of an even thickness. One end will be rounded, but avoid a brisket with a tapered tip. Unlike fattier braising cuts such as short ribs, brisket can get dry without its protective fat cap, which also gives flavor.

HORSERADISH CREAM

¾ cup sour cream

1 tbsp prepared horseradish

coarse salt and freshly ground black pepper

- Mix the sour cream with the horseradish (like Gold's, sold in the refrigerator case) and salt and pepper to taste.

PICKLED ONION

1 red onion, thinly sliced

½ cup red wine vinegar

⅓ cup sugar

1 cinnamon stick

½ tbsp whole black peppercorns

1 chile de árbol, broken in half

1 bay leaf

- Put the onion in a heatproof bowl. In a nonreactive pot, bring 1 cup water, the vinegar, sugar, cinnamon stick, peppercorns, chile de árbol, and bay leaf to a boil and then pour over the onion. Let cool completely and refrigerate.

CONTINUED FROM

MEAT LOAF

Michael Symon | Lola | Cleveland

NOBODY ROLLS OUT A MEAT LOAF to the table for holidays or festive meals. Most feasts are ruled by those huge baked orbs: turkey and ham. But skip those once in a while. Pound for pound, neither one—despite the hours in the oven and all that carving—can match a good meat loaf in intensity of flavor and crowd-pleasing potential. The rich nuggets of fat in the ground meats seep and bubble throughout it, spreading flavor. (Think of a well-marbled steak.) Meat loaf is beautiful. It's cheap as hell and easy to make. Plus, a few simple rules can lead you to countless variations on the traditional loaf. My philosophy is, you can pull big flavor from simple ingredients if you follow a process. It's all about technique.

SERVES 4 TO 6

DIFFICULTY:

EASY | REASONABLE | WORTH THE EFFORT

blended olive oil (see **Note, page 139**)

1 tbsp unsalted butter

1 red onion, finely diced (about 1 cup)

3 cloves garlic, minced

1½ lb coarsely ground beef (preferably with 20 percent fat)

1½ lb hot Italian pork sausage, removed from casings

2 tbsp chopped fresh cilantro

2 eggs, beaten

1 cup panko (Japanese bread crumbs)

coarse salt and freshly ground black pepper to taste

- Preheat the oven to 375°F. Oil a 9-by-5-inch loaf pan or a shallow roasting pan with the olive oil.

- Melt the butter in small skillet over medium heat and cook the onion and garlic until translucent. Let cool.

- Put all the remaining ingredients and the onion mixture in a large bowl and mix with your hands. Put the mixture in the prepared pan, pressing down and packing medium tight (or mold into a meat-loaf shape and place in a roasting pan). Bake for 40 minutes or until it reaches an internal temperature of 170°F. Remove from the pan, slice, and serve.

TIP: You can make a truckload of these weeks in advance. Make one at a time, and let the pan cool between baking. Freeze unsliced.

UNNATURAL THOUGHTS ON
THE WAGYU

WHAT DOES IT MEAN WHEN MEAT COSTS $130 A POUND?

By Tom Junod

A DOZEN YEARS AGO, I went to a slaughterhouse. I parked next to the space reserved for the "kill floor employee of the month," took a breath that I never succeeded in letting out, and went in. I had to put on a raincoat and high rubber boots before joining the line—meatpackers dress like firemen, with matronly hairnets taking the place of heroic helmets—and was glad I did. The stuff on the floor wasn't *deep* or anything like that, but there was definitely stuff on the floor, and I was definitely glad to be insulated from it. There was also, more ineffably, stuff in the air—a subtle bronze shading, a particulate mist—and I was glad to be insulated from it as well. What I couldn't be insulated from, however, was the taste. The smell, awful as it was, pervasive and inti-

mate as it was, could be avoided if you didn't breathe. I didn't breathe. The taste, however, took advantage of something I couldn't control, something that was the infernal place's entire reason for being: my hunger. The long pink tongues hanging from hooks, like some killer clown's idea of a tie rack; the leering heads, excavated of eyes but not of ears; the near-calves, freed from the slit wombs to sprawl lifelessly on the floor: They all exuded a flavor, and it was the flavor of steak. A grotesque parody of steak, to be sure, the succulent fats turned to rancid grease on my tongue, the salty blood like a coating of copper, the deep-red flesh as strong as offal. And yet I couldn't resist. The taste in my mouth filled my mouth and made its way down my throat, as if some forcibly disembodied cow-conscience had issued a challenge: You call yourself a carnivore? You call yourself a meat eater? All right, then: Eat up!

It took a while to recover. The burning images went away first; I just blinked my eyes and tried not to remember. The smell went away after a week's worth of obsessive showering. The taste, though, stayed right where it was, the distillation of the death I'd witnessed coming suddenly alive every time I ate a piece of fish or a joint of chicken or an abstemious green salad. I wasn't eating beef, of course; indeed, I was deciding whether to eat the meat culled from cows ever again and couldn't imagine when I would find it within myself to take a knife to my daily allotment of protein and draw blood not so different from my own. Then I had to do an interview at a steakhouse. It was with a scientist who had not only created new forms of life—chimerical combinations of sheep and cows, for instance—but who had concluded his experiments by butchering and eating them. He knew all about slaughterhouses; he'd gotten some of the raw material for his science at slaughterhouses, and when I told him that I'd just been to a slaughterhouse, he insisted that we do the interview at a Longhorn. He was that kind of guy, impish, and he wanted me to make a decision, and to make it right in front of him. He was watching me when the waitress came around and delivered the menus. Of course, you don't really need a menu at a Longhorn, or at any steakhouse—that's why they exist. You know what you want. He was like, "Well?" And so I ordered a steak; I ordered the flesh. It just seemed odd not to, even after what I'd seen, *especially* after what I'd seen. I mean, so many cows dying, and dying horribly—they're dying for me, and suddenly I'm not going to eat them so I can *feel better about myself*? Suddenly I'm going to *pass*? I'd just been made privy to one of life's most terrible secrets—hey, don't kid yourself about the nature of humanity: We're the species that does *this*—and to refuse it based on some idea

I mean, so many cows dying, and dying horribly— they're dying for me, and suddenly I'm not going to eat them so I can feel better about myself?

that we're something else seemed like a willful fudging of the facts, like a decision to stay in the dark. So I ate the steak. And it was not only delicious, all the fat and all the blood and all the flesh in the perfect alignment, it was the proverbial hair of the dog. Eating the product of the slaughterhouse drove the slaughterhouse taste right out of my mouth. I was *cured*, man: I didn't have to think about the taste of murdered cow anymore, because I was eating steak again, and steak tasted good.

The Wagyu came sealed in plastic. I'd ordered it on a Friday, and it came to my house on a Saturday, unfrozen but prophylactically pure, and for a day or so I just watched it in my refrigerator, as if it were sushi that had been delivered in its own aquarium. It was beautiful, and the plastic served a purpose that I believed was Wagyu's purpose: to interpose a layer of separation between me and the reality of what I was eating, to make it seem like I was eating something else besides clobbered cow. Wagyu is a program of transcendence, after all. Wagyu cattle are worshipped before they are killed. They are bred so that fat corrupts the striations of every muscle, fed a smorgasbord of grains that starving children would envy, raised on a regimen of sloth to rid their flesh of any residue of resistance, then ritualistically delivered to their fate. I left it in the fridge because I didn't want to sully it with my appetite. I left it in the fridge because, like so many things originating in the extremity of Japanese culture, Wagyu was a decadence that required fanatical application of the will, and eating it was like eating a fattened monk.

Now, my Wagyu was American Wagyu, but that's almost a contradiction in terms. Since when does America turn its beef into something akin to truffles? When does America do anything with its beef but democratize it and make it the culinary equivalent of the two-car garage? American Wagyu was like bonsai sequoia. It was the American Beauty rose, hothoused into the genital splendor of the orchid. It was the supermarket staple, made not only new but foreign. It wasn't even red meat. It was magenta. For an estimated cost of $200, I'd received two steaks totaling about two pounds—a spool of skirt and a porterhouse. The skirt steak was lovely, wound conically under its sheath of plastic, like a child's toy you could eat. The porterhouse was garish. It was pretty as porn stars are pretty. It wasn't swirled with fat the way supermarket steaks are; it was flecked with it, the fat distributed the way iron filings are distributed by a magnet. There was a flickering universe of fat in that steak, and so it wasn't something that could be excised with a steak knife and left behind like a rind on the plate. The fat was pervasive and widespread, as inescapable as the symbolism.

> . . . it had a smell, a strong smell, not just beefy but gamey, a violent smell almost, redolent not of pacific pastures but of predatory pursuit.

I unsealed the Wagyu—always referred to as a singular entity, because eating it is supposed to be a singular experience—after two days. It was grainy to the touch, with its photons of fat. Its blood was syrupy, like good balsamic vinegar, as if it had already been reduced at the bottom of a pan. And it had a smell, a strong smell, not just beefy but gamey, a violent smell almost, redolent not of pacific pastures but of predatory pursuit. It freaked me out a little, to tell the truth, because I was expecting the Wagyu to deliver me *from* the reality of beef; instead, it was delivering me into it. I hadn't smelled anything remotely as strong as Wagyu since . . . well, since I didn't want to say. I was having friends over, and I didn't want to ruin their appetites. So I shut up, got the grill going, massaged the steaks with salt and pepper and a little olive oil, and prepared to put flesh to fire. The Wagyu had come with all sorts of caveats concerning its cooking. The meat eater was instructed to honor the meat he was eating, was warned to avoid the sin—and yes, it was put in those terms, as though congregants at the temple of Wagyu had to beware the money changers—of overcooking. As it turns out, the stuff was nearly impervious to heat. Of course, the skirt went on

and off the Weber in the time it took me to get beer from the refrigerator. But if the lure of the grill is that it offers reenactment of an ancient practice, the lure of the Wagyu porterhouse was that it offered something new, and did something I'd never seen steak do before. It didn't brown; it bronzed. It golded. The fatty flesh immediately formed a uniform gold crust, as if in advertisement of its own unholy cost, and then sort of stopped cooking. I kept thinking to myself, *Hey, I'm cooking the shit out of this poor beast*, and then every time I took a knife to it, the gash was like a raw wound. One was instructed to cook the Wagyu like ahi tuna; the porterhouse, however, had a mind of its own. It was so dense inside that it stayed cold underneath its sizzling precious-metal shell, stayed purple, stayed heart-colored. I sliced it, served it, and thought the question it would force me to contend with was: Do I want to eat beef that has been turned, by human intervention, into something other than beef? Did I want to eat beef that acted like ahi tuna?

I needn't have worried. The Wagyu was beef, all right. It didn't taste like ahi; nor did it taste like foie gras, which is another of its advertised equivalencies. The problem was that it didn't taste like steak, either. It didn't taste like the familiar thing we know of as steak. Well, the skirt steak did, more or less; it was delicious, though so tender—so buttery—that it tasted somehow *softened*, like an overripe plum. The porterhouse, though, packed a wallop like a French whore's armpit. It delivered a blast of intimacy—with the cow, and with the process by which the cow was delivered to the table—that was, to say the least, unwelcome. I kept looking around at my fellow diners like the emperor trying on his new clothes. I wanted to say, right away, Hey, do you guys actually *like* this? Instead I watched them eat. I watched the porterhouse disappear, engulfed not only by appetite but by the expectation of appetite. For my brother and my friend Vince's girlfriend, eating the Wagyu started as an indulgence, then lightened into a kind of meat snack. They polished off slice after slice of wine-dark porterhouse. For me and for Vince, it was the other way around. We were instantly sated. I caught his eye across the table, and his eyes were rolling, like those of a man pushing incalculable weight. Finally, he said, "This is *intense*," which my eager ears took to mean: This tastes like death itself. And it did. The Wagyu owed its density to the density of death itself. A dozen years ago, I'd gotten a taste of the slaughterhouse and had worked ever since to free myself of that mortal tang, cheap cut by cheap cut, steak by undistinguished steak. Now I was eating steak that cost $130 a pound, and instead of being steak that transcended the slaughterhouse, it functioned as a slaughterhouse *madeleine*. Indeed, as I ate the Wagyu, I did something I hadn't done since the slaughterhouse, at least not in response to the reality of beef. I remembered what I was eating, in the most visceral way. And I gagged.

I made a decision to continue eating beef after going to the slaughterhouse. It was a decision that I felt I'd earned the right to make, after taking full measure of the abyss—an existential decision of sorts, because I was no longer consuming beef passively, out of ignorance, but rather actively, in the face of awful enlightenment. There was nothing the most militant vegetarian could tell me that I didn't already know. There was no vein of disgust that I hadn't already tapped and tasted. I was choosing to eat beef, in part, to *triumph* over disgust, not to mention sympathy and scruple. I was choosing to eat beef as a hungry American, in affirmation of both my appetite and of America in general. By choosing the death of the cow—sorry, the cows; the vast, bellowing multitudes of cows—I was choosing life, or at least the life I knew, the carnivorous one, the supermarket one, the democratic one. Sure, I liked how cow tasted. But in the end I chose to keep eating dead cows because I believed I'd earned the right to exercise the right—the American right—to keep tasting them.

> I kept looking around at my fellow diners like the emperor trying on his new clothes. I wanted to say, right away, Hey, do you guys actually *like* this?

Do we have the right to eat Wagyu? A lot of things have changed in a dozen years, after all. The American awareness has changed. We're aware of our limitations as no Americans have been since the Great Depression, and we're also aware of our inability to stop trying to transcend them. We were the country that never turned around to see the frowns on the jugglers and the clowns when they all did tricks for us; now the frowns are all we see, and yet we are helpless to get up and walk away from the show. We know damn well that beef is a grotesquerie, and that its production, in factory feedlots and pitiless slaughterhouses, is an evil. We know that it is wasteful in terms of resources, promiscuous in terms of carbon footprint, and insulting to our self-image as citizens of a sustainable planet. We know this and we respond with . . . Wagyu! We respond by going superprime in the age of subprime. We respond with the Hummer of beef, the hedge fund of beef, the foie gras of beef, whose taste made me feel as force-fed as the unfortunate geese who donate their livers to our tasting menus. We respond with beef that costs ten times or twenty times as much as mass-market beef, so that we can eat something that tastes uncomfortably of, well, *beef*. Do we have the right to eat Wagyu? Of *course* we have the right to eat Wagyu. We are trapped by our right to eat Wagyu. We will continue eating Wagyu until there is no more Wagyu, unless we find the courage to renounce Wagyu. Do we, as a society, have the political will to renounce Wagyu? I do. I renounce Wagyu. It would be a different story if I liked Wagyu, if the taste of Wagyu didn't make me want to hurl, just as it would be a different story if I actually owned a Hummer. But I don't. I renounce the obvious extremity so I can still, somehow, embrace the ingrained extremity of American life. I renounce the Hummer so I can go on driving my BMW station wagon. And I renounce Wagyu, so that I can forget the slaughterhouse once and for all, and go back to eating steak.

BEEF STEW

with Ale

Bryan Voltaggio | Volt | Frederick, Maryland

A GOOD STEW TAKES TIMING: putting ingredients in the pot in the correct order to make sure everything is finished at the same time. This is my go-to hunting-camp dish, because after prepping everything at home, I can put it together in one pot and then sit around the fire until it's done, drinking and bullshitting—which is 90 percent of hunting anyway. A few other bits of stew wisdom: Always cut your own stew meat. You never know which bits and pieces are thrown into that precut "stew meat" pile at the store, but you can be sure it's a lot of tough, dry odds and ends. Dusting the meat with Wondra flour—which is easier to work with than regular flour—will help keep the meat from sticking and adds a thick, luscious finish to the stew. As for the vegetables, the ones I use are large, solid, and easy to square off. After they're peeled, just lop off one end so it sits flat and have at it. As chefs, we're always using a touch of acid to wake flavors up—think of how a squeeze of lime transforms a vodka tonic. Flavors can become muted in dishes that cook for a long time; a bit of the malt vinegar I use here is a little slap in its face.

SERVES 4 TO 6

DIFFICULTY:

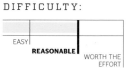

EASY | REASONABLE | WORTH THE EFFORT

2 lb beef brisket, trimmed and cut into 2-inch chunks

coarse salt and freshly ground black pepper

about 2 tbsp Wondra flour

about 5 tbsp canola oil

2 large portobello mushrooms, wiped clean, stemmed, and diced

2 cloves garlic, chopped

1½ cups white or red pearl onions (about 8 oz)

1 cup diced carrots (2 medium)

1 cup diced celeriac (celery root; 1 medium)

1 cup diced rutabaga or turnip (1 large)

2 bottles brown lager or brown ale

2 cups beef broth or stock

1 cup chopped Yukon gold potatoes

3 tsp malt vinegar

leaves from 4 sprigs fresh thyme

leaves from 2 small sprigs fresh rosemary, coarsely chopped

CONTINUED

- Generously season all sides of the beef with salt and pepper and lightly dust with the Wondra flour.

- Add the canola oil to a Dutch oven and place over high heat. When the oil is almost smoking (or shimmering in the pan), brown the meat in small batches, turning to sear all sides and removing each batch as it is finished. When all the brisket is browned and removed from the pot, add the mushrooms and cook in the residual beef fat until browned. Add the garlic and cook, stirring frequently, until just softened (but not colored), about 3 minutes. Remove with a slotted spoon and set aside.

- Add onions, carrots, celeriac, and rutabaga and cook, stirring frequently, allowing the onion to brown, about 10 minutes. Remove the vegetables. Return the beef to the pot and add the lager. Bring to a boil, then reduce the heat, skimming any fat from the surface using a spoon or ladle. Cook to reduce the beer by two thirds, about 8 minutes. (Pay attention—it'll reduce quickly.) Add the beef broth. Cover and simmer over very low heat until the meat is starting to become tender—about 1 hour—then add the potatoes and the browned vegetables. Check the stew after another hour: If simmering very slowly, the meat should be fork-tender at this point. Add the vinegar and adjust the seasoning to taste. Stir in the herbs and the mushrooms and cook to heat through. Serve.

CONTINUED FROM

THE
PORK
ANGEL

By David Curcurito

MY PARENTS WERE DIVORCED and my mom was out running the bowling alley every night, so I never learned to cook. It was the early '80s, and microwavable meals were new. I pretty much lived on those until I was eighteen. I was like a stray dog. So over the years, the women I've dated who could cook were different. Special. They nurtured me. Even if their cooking wasn't good, it was wonderful.

Now I have a house out in the country, with a kitchen that's just huge—too big for a man who can't cook. It has twenty-foot ceilings and a counter big enough to play Ping-Pong on. A few years and two girlfriends ago, this kitchen found its soul. Just before Thanksgiving—neither of us had anywhere to be—she proposed cooking a suckling pig at the house. This sounded excellent, but I had no idea what it meant, so I got nervous as hell. I went out to the house a day ahead and scrubbed the place like it was an operating room. Meanwhile, back in Manhattan, this living saint of a woman was beginning her journey. She bought the pig—she was the kind of woman who knew where to buy a pig—packed it in a bag with ice, and stuffed it into her rolling suitcase. Then she took the subway to Port Authority, boarded a bus for High Falls, New York, and rode for an hour and a half with that pig in the suitcase on a rack above her seat. When she stepped off the bus, I felt as if she were stepping off a plane from China with our adopted child. I felt like a father when the newborn arrives home—I should have hung a sign that said, "Welcome Home, Suckling Pig."

In the kitchen, all I could do was watch as she tore open the bag and started preparing. She cooked that pig until it was golden brown and the meat inside was like silk. We tore into it like coyotes eating a fresh kill. We ate the ears, we ate its face. We ate everything. I felt loved.

GRILLED DOUBLE-CUT PORK CHOP
and Braised Cabbage

David Katz | Mémé | Philadelphia

MY DAD GRILLED outside year-round—weather didn't matter. There could be snow on the ground, and he still wouldn't pull anything off the fire until there was charring on the edges. Crusty black charring isn't just a look, it's a smell—a smell that means grilling to me. You can get that charring without sacrificing moistness by grilling a double-cut chop (rather than two single chops), a dish that'll keep you warm till spring. Ask your butcher for a double-cut Berkshire pork chop tied with the fat cap left on.

SERVES 2

DIFFICULTY:

1 double-cut Berkshire pork chop, tied with the fat cap left on

canola oil for brushing

coarse salt and freshly ground black pepper

6 thick strips smoked bacon, chopped

½ large onion, sliced

1 bay leaf

1 Fuji apple, peeled and sliced

4 cups sliced cabbage

one 12-oz bottle Unibroue Éphémère (or wheat beer)

2 pinches fresh thyme leaves

maple syrup for brushing

• Adjust the grill so it's about 3 inches from the heat source and get the coals white-hot. Brush the meat with canola oil, season with salt and pepper, and sear over the hottest coals until browned on both sides. Ideally, you'll turn it only once—so, say, 5 minutes per side.

• Place a heavy enamel pot over medium-hot coals, off to the side. While the meat sears, render the bacon in the pot for about 3 minutes. Add the onion, a pinch of salt and pepper, and the bay leaf. Stir once or twice and cook until the onion softens but doesn't color, about 5 minutes. Add the apple and cook until soft, about 2 minutes. Add the cabbage and stir well to coat. Add the Éphémère (a Canadian ale made with apple) or wheat beer such as Hoegaarden, thyme leaves, and more salt and pepper, and cover.

• Move the chop to indirect heat and close the grill lid, creating an oven. After 15 minutes, open the lid, brush both sides of the chop with maple syrup, uncover the pot (so the ale can evaporate), and close the lid, continuing to cook until the chop is cooked through with a slight edge of pink, about another 15 minutes. (A meat thermometer should read 140° to 145°F.) With a total of 40 to 45 minutes' cooking time, plus the browning action of the sugary syrup, the meat will get a little crusty. But that's good. You want a little love on the edges.

PORK BUTT

By Ted Allen

JUST BECAUSE IT'S A CHEAP SLAB OF PIG DOESN'T MEAN IT AIN'T DELICIOUS.

ASK A MAN WHO KNOWS his meat and he will tell you this: The cheap cuts are some of the best. Any jackass can blow 20 bones a pound on beef tenderloin—silky, yes, but flavorless. You really want to pay top dollar for meat that requires bacon or butter sauce to taste like something? Mario Batali knows his meat. And when he speaks of it, the Iron Chef savors his words as if they themselves were succulent bites: "Bone-in pork shoulder!" he proclaims when asked for his favorite roast. (It's often labeled pork "picnic" or "butt," for some reason, although it is not from the ass end of things.) "You'll never find it in Chinatown, because it's the first piece of meat to go," Batali says. "You'll always find it in white-guy town, because it's the last to go." And, deliciously, it runs about $2.50 a pound. You just have to know how to cook the thing. Like many inexpensive meats, this portion of pig is full of marbling and connective tissue that make for tough going unless you cook it a long time. But after a few hours of low heat, the fat (read: juicy flavor) melts gorgeously into the flesh.

Myself, I'm partial to the Puerto Rican style, a traditional Sunday dish called *pernil*: Stabbed all over with a paring knife, slathered in olive oil, garlic, salt, and oregano, marinated for a day, and then slow roasted, it perfumes the house (and half the neighborhood) with wondrousness and yields a succulent, crisp-on-the-outside, fall-off-the-bone roast. (That's the other thing: You do want the bone in. More flavor.)

In the Batali house, says Mr. Molto, "we do it like a *porchetta*," that is, like a Tuscan-style suckling pig. He rubs the meat with fennel seeds, garlic, and rosemary, puts it in a 250°F oven—and he goes to bed. "Then I wake up and take it out," he says. "You need it to go eight hours. Then it needs to sit in its own juices—and just sit there—until it cools. Later, you reheat it in the same pan and carve it, and there's nothing better."

PORK SHOULDER

alla Porchetta

Mario Batali | Del Posto | New York City

SERVES 6 TO 8

DIFFICULTY:

| EASY | REASONABLE | WORTH THE EFFORT |

4 lb boneless pork shoulder (pork butt)

coarse salt and freshly ground black pepper

¼ cup extra-virgin olive oil

1 onion, thinly sliced

1 bulb fennel, fronds chopped and reserved, bulb thinly sliced

2 lb ground pork shoulder (you can use already-made sausages if need be)

2 tbsp fennel seeds

2 tbsp freshly ground black pepper

2 tbsp chopped fresh rosemary

6 cloves garlic, thinly sliced

2 eggs, beaten

4 red onions, halved

- Preheat the oven to 350°F. Have your butcher butterfly the pork shoulder to an even 1-inch thickness; you should have a flat piece of meat about 8 inches by 14 inches. Sprinkle with salt and pepper and set aside.

- In a sauté pan, heat the olive oil until smoking. Add the onion and fennel bulb and sauté until softened and lightly browned, about 10 minutes. Add the ground pork, fennel seeds, pepper, rosemary, and garlic and cook until the meat turns a light color, stirring constantly, about 10 minutes. Allow to cool. Add the chopped fennel leaves and eggs and mix well.

- Spread the mixture over the pork and roll up like a jelly roll. Tie with butcher's twine and place in a roasting pan on top of the red onions. Place in the oven and roast for 2½ hours, until the internal temperature reaches 160°F. Remove and allow to rest for 10 to 20 minutes. Cut into 1-inch-thick pieces and serve.

WHAT I'VE **LEARNED** MARIO BATALI

CHEF, NEW YORK CITY

Interviewed by Cal Fussman, 2004

God is fat. God's also skinny. God's also Linda Evangelista. God's a lot of things.

Who ordered all this stuff? Oh, yeah. Me.

Food is much better off the hand than the fork.

My first memory? I can't remember. But I can remember being almost five, sitting on a swing, and wondering how many times I was going to sit on a swing in my life. Of course I didn't realize it at that moment, but what I was really wondering was, How long can I stay young?

I can tell in two minutes if I should hire someone in the kitchen. Two minutes. It's his desire. It's that open-eyed, attentive expression. If he doesn't have it . . . I mean, I can teach a chimp how to cook dinner. But I cannot teach a chimp how to love it.

I come from an Italian family. One of the greatest and most profound expressions we would ever use in conversations or arguments was a slamming door. The slamming door was our punctuation mark.

If you want your kids to listen to you, don't yell at them. Whisper. Make them lean in. My kids taught me that. And I do it with adults now.

What do I love about New York? Eight million people can hate my restaurant, and there's still eight million left! Not that I want to piss anyone off. But it gives you a lot of chances to work on your game.

Some people don't care about food. They eat the same thing every day. But I can change that. Can you make a celibate horny? Oh, yeah. You just need to find out what he's hiding from.

A great friend is someone who gives what you want to take and takes what you want to give.

I don't know about those personal trainers. They seem to be for people who don't have enough domination in their lives.

A little piece of watermelon on top of a magnificent piece of raw tuna in the middle of summer makes a lot of sense— as long as you put some salt on it.

Have I ever seen it on somebody's face? Oh, yeah. The worst case was Gael Greene, *New York* magazine food critic. I'm working at a place called Rocco's in the Village. We were kind of warned that she was coming in, and we were ready. I'm cooking with one other guy. Six people order appetizers. Boom. Boom. Boom. Steamed mussels. I'm putting them all on the plate, and as they're going out, I get a whiff. Something's wrong. These mussels smell like shit. It wasn't that they were spoiled; they were in their mating season. They give off this weird smell. I go running out after them just as they're placed in front of her. She smells them and just waves them away. God, I'll never forget it.

Holding back is the hardest thing for a cook to do, especially in a multicourse meal. Because the cook is battling what makes him a great cook. The cook wants to give. Here it is! And that's a hard thing to control. You don't realize that by seven courses, the diner's ready to vomit.

You sit down at Katz's and you eat the big bowl of pickles and you're eating the pastrami sandwich, and halfway through you say to yourself, I should really wrap this up and save it for tomorrow. But the sandwich is calling you: Remember the taste you just had. So fatty. It's what you want. It's what you are! I've never gotten home from Katz's with a doggie bag in my hand. A pastrami sandwich at Katz's is what's bad and good about food. It's the sacred and the profane.

Escarole in December is not escarole in January.

Flexibility, tolerance, thoughtfulness, love—that's what makes a marriage work. But love goes away quickly when kids are around for a while. There are going to be days when the love in your relationship becomes a secondary factor. It'll come back. So you hold on. What choice do you have?

It's not like I'm megalomaniacally opening up restaurants. The truth is, I can't stop. Because ever since I've been in New York City, which is twelve years, every time I've run into a good person, I've said, "Stick with me and one day you'll get a slice of the pie." At this point, the slices are starting to be handed out. I'm like an Italian grandmother who's been watching her grandchildren learn to ride on the old family bicycle. When they can ride it with no hands, they're ready for a new bike.

If you're smart, then your dreams evolve too.

My last meal? The food would be much less significant than the company.

You want a little more wine?

ESQUIRE
Classics

PRETTY EASY RECIPES FOR SOME OF THE BEST BURGERS OF ALL TIME.

Reprinted from the *Esquire Cookbook*, 1955

BURGER VARIATIONS

HAMBURGERS

The superlative hamburger starts at your meat market, where you firmly refuse all ready-chopped meat and pick out a handsome slab of top or bottom round or top sirloin. Have it carefully trimmed of all outer fat; in some markets, the only way you can convince a butcher that you want the meat lean is to tell him you intend to eat it raw. Then have it put through the chopper only once. Handle the meat as gently as you can when you're seasoning and shaping it, and cook it as soon as possible after the grinding. (The ideal is to grind it yourself, just before cooking, but that very nearly requires an electric gadget; the ordinary hand-operated meat grinder is apt to mangle the meat.) Allow $^{1}/_{2}$ pound per person if you're going to cook the meat in its pristine form, with nothing but a little seasoning to point it up. But if your recipe calls for bread and other additions, figure a pound of meat to feed 3 or 4 people.

How will you cook your hamburgers? Quickly—in a heavy skillet sizzling with a bit of butter, or in your oiled broiler, or over a bit of charcoal fire. Remember mainly that hamburgers cook in a hurry, and dry out when overcooked. If you like them rare, they're done almost as soon as they're brown. If you want them cooked through, reduce the heat after they're handsomely browned; finish the cooking at a slower clip.

HAMBURGER LUCHOW

For 8, have your butcher grind 3 pounds of lean top round with $^{1}/_{2}$ pound beef marrow. (If he hasn't that much marrow, have him make up the difference with fresh kidney fat.) Trim crusts from $^{1}/_{2}$ pound bread and soak bread in water to soften. Squeeze out water, break bread into bits, and mix with the meat; add salt and pepper, a trifle of nutmeg, 2 raw eggs, and a few teaspoons of water. Form into patties and fry, sauté, or broil, as desired.

HAMBURGERS BURGUNDY

Brown quickly in hot butter ground top sirloin or round steak patties. When meat is brown, add 3 tablespoons Burgundy to the pan, plus a pinch of chervil and a pinch of marjoram. Cover and simmer for 1 minute. Serve at once.

BARBECUED HAMBURGERS

Finely dice 1 onion; mix with 2 beaten eggs, salt, and pepper; blend gently into 2 pounds freshly ground bottom round. Form into cakes. Slice a long loaf of French bread thinly at an angle; butter on one side and toast very lightly. Grill hamburgers, basting once on each side with a mildly spicy barbecue sauce. Serve with assorted relishes, plus a platter of tomato quarters. And red wine.

HAMBURGERS WITH ALLSPICE

Devotees of this method claim that a genuine hamburger is always seasoned with freshly ground allspice. To judge for yourself you'll need some whole allspice, a pepper mill to grind the brown berries in, and a chunk of lean beef. Grind the beef fine with a small onion; the onion is merely a seasoning and must not dominate the flavor. Grind a good supply of allspice on the beef, add salt and a very little pepper, mix well, pat the mixture into cakes, and fry them in butter. When the hamburgers are cooked, remove them to a hot platter. Into the butter remaining in the pan, grind a small issue of allspice. Stir and cook for 30 seconds, then pour the perfumed butter over the burgers or the accompanying mashed potatoes.

HAMBURGER BALLS

To I pound of ground beef, add I beaten egg, 2 tablespoons sour cream, 1/4 cup minced onion, 2 to 3 tablespoons chopped parsley, 1/2 cup bread crumbs, I teaspoon salt, 1/4 teaspoon pepper, and a pinch of thyme. Blend and form into 4 big balls. Butter a heavy oven pan with 2 tablespoons butter, place the hamburgers therein, and top each with 1/2 teaspoon beef bouillon. Place under the broiler; broil for 6 minutes on one side, turn, and broil 4 minutes on the other side. Remove meat to hot platter. Add 4 tablespoons boiling water to the pan, scrape and stir up the drippings; add 1/2 cup heavy cream, blend, and pour over hamburgers. Place hamburgers on large toasted, buttered sandwich buns, flank with assorted pickles, and serve. With beer.

MINIATURE HAMBURGERS

Have I ounce of suet ground in with I pound of bottom round. To the meat add a pinch of basil, I tablespoon chopped parsley (fresh or dried), I tablespoon finely minced scallions, salt, freshly ground pepper, and 2 tablespoons red wine. Mix carefully, form into tiny thin cakes about the size of baking powder biscuits, and brush cakes lightly with mustard. Let the cakes age in the refrigerator for at least 6 hours. When dinnertime approaches, make a pan of small biscuits; try the prepared kind that require only baking. Brown the hamburgers momentarily in hot butter and serve ceremoniously on hot buttered biscuits.

BEERBURGERS

For 4, mix 2 pounds of ground beef with I tablespoon grated onion, I teaspoon salt, and 1/2 teaspoon pepper. Shape into 8 thick patties. Heat 2 tablespoons fat in a large, heavy skillet and brown the patties on both sides. While they're browning, mix well the following sauce: 1/2 cup catsup, 1/2 cup beer, 2 tablespoons each of vinegar, sugar, and Worcestershire sauce, I teaspoon salt, and 1/8 teaspoon pepper. When the patties are brown, pour the sauce over them and simmer for 10 minutes. When they're about ready for the table, slice French bread at an angle into thin oval pieces. Butter on one side and toast slightly. Place the burgers on the bread and ladle the remaining sauce over them.

HAMBURGER HARRIGAN

Mash I clove garlic in 1/2 teaspoon salt; stir in and blend I tablespoon Worcestershire sauce, I dash Tabasco sauce, I tablespoon olive oil, and 3 tablespoons claret. Mix with I pound hamburger meat and form into round cakes, handling as little as possible. Refrigerate for a couple of hours, then fry or broil. No additional seasoning is needed. Serve with toasted rolls, mustard, catsup, chili, relish, sliced onions, and beer.

THE INSIDE STRAIGHT HAMBURGER

Rub a mixing bowl with a cut clove of garlic. In the bowl, blend prime ground beef with assorted herbs, salt, and pepper, a little mustard, and I tablespoon red wine. Form thick cakes, sized to fit neatly on thick crustless slices of Italian bread (the round loaf). Fry the hamburgers in butter, place them on a hot platter, and pop into a warming oven until all preparations are completed. Add 1/4 pound butter to the frying pan and drop in: I to 3 teaspoons Worcestershire sauce, I tablespoon finely chopped chives, 3 tablespoons diced mushrooms, and 3 tablespoons red wine. Stir the mixture briskly as it comes to a boil. Correct seasoning and remove pan from fire. Dip each slice of bread quickly into the sauce, on one side only, then top with a hamburger and serve with the usual condiments and mustards. Partners: cole slaw and cold ale.

SOUTH-OF-THE-BORDER HAMBURGER

To I pound of ground beef, add I teaspoon chili powder, I tablespoon onion juice, I teaspoon red wine vinegar, I tablespoon olive oil, salt, and a turn of the pepper mill. Form into thick portions and grill, preferably over hot coals, basting twice with a mixture of melted butter and lime juice in equal proportions. Slip the cakes between halves of flat, lightly toasted, generously buttered sandwich buns. Pink Mexican beans and tomato slices in French dressing go well.

Garlic-Rosemary Roasted
PICNIC HAM

Michael White | Marea | New York City

THE FIRST TIME I HAD FRESH picnic ham, I was twenty-one, working as a chef in Imola, Italy. On a day off we went to the Formula One racetrack. In Italy, this type of stuff is their "ballpark food"—their version of a hot dog. They put freshly roasted whole pigs smeared with garlic and rosemary on trucks and head out to the speedways. You walk up to the truck and they hand you a slice they've just cut, topped with a piece of crackly skin. I love to make this on Sundays to eat throughout the week, but it usually doesn't last past Monday. I use the shank end of a fresh pork leg—also called a fresh ham—because the dark and white meat and the connective tissue give you a robust pork flavor. Ask your butcher to score the fat for you—it'll keep it from curling up. Or you can score it yourself by cutting a crosshatch pattern into the skin with an X-Acto knife. This dish is really hard to mess up—the skin protects the meat from drying out, so you'd have to really try to overcook it.

SERVES 8 TO 10

DIFFICULTY:

EASY | REASONABLE | WORTH THE EFFORT

HERBED SALT MIX

¼ cup chopped fresh rosemary

2 tbsp chopped fresh sage

2 tbsp fennel seeds, toasted

3 cloves garlic

grated zest of 2 lemons

1 cup kosher salt

1 tbsp freshly ground black pepper

HAM

1 fresh ham (see Tip), 8 to 10 lb

1 cup olive oil, plus more for drizzling

- TO MAKE THE HERBED SALT MIX: Combine all the ingredients in a food processor and buzz together until green.

- Preheat the oven to 325°F. Place about 1 inch of water in the bottom of a big roasting pan fitted with a rack. Brush the ham with olive oil and season liberally with the herbed salt mix. (Cover and save the extra mix in the refrigerator for up to 1 month.) Place the ham on roasting-pan rack and put in the oven. Cook until the skin is golden and crackling and the internal temperature at the bone is 160°F, 2½ to 3 hours (18 to 22 minutes per pound).

- Remove from the oven, cover lightly with foil, and let rest for at least 20 minutes. Slice and eat with a drizzle of olive oil and extra herbed salt.

  TIP: Fresh ham, also known as fresh pork leg, is the uncured hind leg of the pig. Ask for it with the bone in and skin on.

Berkshire
PORK RIB ROAST

Zach Bell | Cafe Boulud | Palm Beach, Florida

A PORK RACK IS AS REGAL a centerpiece as a beef rib roast, but it doesn't break the bank. The quick curing here penetrates and seals the meat with an undercurrent of whatever flavor you add—in this case, pepper and herbes de Provence. (About those herbs: As a chef, I usually promote fresh herbs, but herbes de Provence is the one dried herb I'm proud to have in my pantry. It's a blend of aromatic herbs typical of the South of France, picked at their peak in the summer and meant to be used throughout the year.) The salt does wonders for sealing in the juices, making the already marbled and juicy Berkshire wonderfully obscene.

SERVES 4 TO 8

DIFFICULTY:

EASY	REASONABLE	WORTH THE EFFORT

one 8-bone pork rack, cut from the front of the loin section, bones in (see Tip)

$\frac{1}{2}$ cup coarse salt

$\frac{1}{4}$ cup packed brown sugar

$\frac{1}{4}$ cup freshly ground black pepper, plus more for seasoning

$\frac{1}{4}$ cup herbes de Provence

olive oil for brushing

Dijon mustard for serving

- Rinse the rack of pork, pat dry, and place in a baking dish. Combine the salt, brown sugar, $\frac{1}{4}$ cup pepper, and herbs in a bowl. Rub the cure liberally onto the pork and place in the refrigerator for 30 minutes. Turn the pork over and let sit for another half-hour.

- Center a roasting rack in the oven and preheat the oven to 475°F. Thoroughly rinse the pork with lukewarm water (to wash away excess salt) and pat dry with paper towels. Set the meat on the roasting rack. To protect the bones from scorching, wrap the end of each (about 2 inches) with folded-over aluminum foil lightly brushed with olive oil. Give the pork a light brush of olive oil and a healthy grinding of black pepper. Roast for 10 minutes. After that "sizzle," lower the oven temperature to 275°F. For a slightly pink center, continue to cook the roast until an instant-read meat thermometer inserted into the deepest part of the roast reads 135°F, 15 to 18 minutes per pound, or another 1 hour and 15 minutes to $1\frac{1}{2}$ hours.

- Remove the pork from the oven. Do not slice! Allow the meat to rest for 20 to 30 minutes. Transfer to a cutting board and carve into double-chop portions to serve 4 or single portions to serve 6 to 8. In lieu of a sauce or jus, I like a big ol' dollop of good Dijon mustard.

TIP: Ask the butcher to "French" the roast (scrape down the meat and fat from the ends of the bones, leaving the bare ends of the bones exposed); you'll have a 5- to 5½-pound roast. The bare bones look more presentable and also make a great handle.

BAKED POLENTA
with Sausage

Luke Palladino | Luke Palladino | Northfield, New Jersey

I CALL THIS "pasticciata," which means "a big mess" in Italian and usually refers to dishes in which the ingredients are mixed together and baked in a casserole. You can vary the taste of this dish by using different sausage or another semisoft cheese, but one thing that cannot change is the polenta. It must be slow cooked and not instant, which might be faster but tastes like nothing.

SERVES 6 TO 8

DIFFICULTY:

| EASY | REASONABLE | WORTH THE EFFORT |

POLENTA

9 cups water

2 tsp coarse salt

2 tbsp extra-virgin olive oil

3 cups stone-ground yellow cornmeal

¾ cup grated Parmesan cheese

1 tbsp unsalted butter

freshly ground black pepper

• TO MAKE THE POLENTA: Bring the water to a boil in a large, heavy pot. Add the salt and olive oil and reduce the heat until the water is simmering. Rain down the cornmeal over the simmering water, adding it very slowly to control flow and whisking constantly to prevent lumps. (If necessary, stop adding cornmeal from time to time and beat the mixture vigorously.) Set over very low heat, cover, and cook, removing lid to stir every 10 minutes. The polenta will become very thick. After 30 minutes, stir in the Parmesan, butter, and salt and pepper to taste. Remove the pot from the heat and cover, keeping it warm until ready to use.

TIP: The best polenta is stone ground (rather than milled with steel rollers), which has a coarse texture and more corn taste. Much of the cooking technique is done to avoid lumps: Seasoning the water early (as with pasta) and slowly "raining" the polenta into the pot while thoroughly whisking helps. You do have to stir while it's cooking, but the amount required is no big deal—about every 10 minutes or so. Use a long-handled wooden spoon to keep your hand out of the way, because steaming polenta can "splat." That's why you never, ever want it to come to a boil; boiling polenta is like molten lava. Consider that a warning.

SAUSAGE

2 tbsp unsalted butter

4 cloves garlic, chopped

12 fresh sage leaves

2 lb Italian sausage, casings removed

1 cup milk

coarse salt and freshly ground black pepper

- TO MAKE THE SAUSAGE: In a large sauté pan over medium heat, melt the butter until foamy. Sauté the garlic and sage leaves until lightly golden. Add the sausage and stir with a wooden spoon, mashing any chunks, and cook until the pork loses its pink color and the edges are slightly brown. Add the milk, cover, and braise on very low heat until almost no liquid remains, 20 to 25 minutes. Season with salt and pepper.

ASSEMBLY

8 oz Gorgonzola dolce cheese, rind removed, crumbled into large pieces

⅓ cup grated Parmesan cheese

- TO ASSEMBLE THE DISH: Preheat the oven to 400°F. Lightly butter a large (8-quart) casserole or 12-inch skillet. Pour the polenta into the buttered casserole, spooning the sausage on top. Evenly distribute the Gorgonzola and sprinkle the Parmesan over all. Bake uncovered until bubbly and golden brown, about 25 minutes. Remove from the oven and let rest for 10 minutes before serving.

ROAST LEG OF LAMB
with Olive Tapenade

Chris Pandel | The Bristol | Chicago

SERVES 6 TO 8

DIFFICULTY:

EASY | REASONABLE | WORTH THE EFFORT

RUB

1 tbsp coarsely ground black pepper

1 tbsp red pepper flakes

1 fresh bay leaf, chopped

leaves from 4 sprigs fresh thyme

2 tbsp minced fresh rosemary needles

2 tbsp minced fresh mint

1 cup olive oil

¼ cup balsamic vinegar

¼ cup honey

LAMB

one 6-lb semiboneless leg of lamb (see Note)

¼ cup kosher salt

Tapenade (recipe follows)

- TO MAKE THE RUB: Whisk together all the ingredients.

- TO MAKE THE LAMB: Preheat the oven to 400°F. (It's always a good idea to turn on the vent and even crack a window for the searing process, which you're about to perform.) Coat the lamb with the rub—making sure you get lots of spices and herbs onto the meat—and sprinkle the roast with kosher salt. (You will probably only use about half the rub mixture; reserve remainder and use it as a dressing on salad greens to make fantastic sandwiches with leftover lamb.) Place the lamb on a rack in a roasting pan and sear in oven for 20 minutes. Reduce the oven temperature to 325°F and roast until a meat thermometer inserted in the thickest part (and away from the bone) reads 130° to 135°F for medium-rare. Allow about 15 to 18 minutes per pound and begin checking after 1½ hours.

- Remove and loosely cover the roast with aluminum foil, allowing the lamb to rest for 30 minutes.

- Carve the roast and serve with tapenade.

NOTE: Most butchers will have semiboneless lamb leg, formed by removing the aitchbone and tying that section of lamb to make it easier to carve.

TAPENADE

1/2 cup minced brine-cured black olives, such as Gaeta

1/4 cup minced drained capers

2 cloves garlic, minced

2 anchovy fillets, minced

2 tbsp minced fresh basil

2 tbsp minced fresh flat-leaf parsley

2 tbsp minced fresh thyme

2 tbsp minced fresh oregano

2 cups olive oil

kosher salt to taste

- TO MAKE THE TAPENADE: Combine all the ingredients in a bowl and stir to blend.

Makes about 2 cups.

CHILAQUILES

Ryan Poli | Perennial | Chicago

SERVES 1 OR 2

DIFFICULTY:

EASY | REASONABLE | WORTH THE EFFORT

chopped garlic to taste

chopped onions to taste

2 tsp olive oil

2 or 3 handfuls corn tortilla chips

1 cup salsa

1 handful shredded Cheddar cheese or Monterey Jack

2 large eggs

- Preheat the broiler. If you have some garlic and onions, chop and fry them up with olive oil in a 10-inch skillet. If not, doesn't matter.

- Give a few handfuls of corn tortilla chips a good soaking in a cup of salsa, so they're just soft. Add them to the skillet and top with a layer of shredded cheese. Crack the eggs over the top and slide the skillet under the broiler until the eggs set and the chips get brown. The chips may char a little on the edges, but they'll taste wet and crunchy, and that's a beautiful thing.

ESQUIRE
Classics

PRETTY EASY RECIPES FOR SOME OF THE BEST BEEF DISHES OF ALL TIME.

Reprinted from the *Esquire Cookbook*, 1955

BEEF STROGANOFF

Three ways to make this Russian favorite.

ONE: Cut 1½ pounds beef fillet into 1-inch squares and season with salt, pepper, and lemon juice. Let stand 1½ hours. Mince 1 onion and sauté it in 1½ tablespoons butter; add 1 cup fresh sliced mushrooms. Cover and simmer until tender. Meantime, shake beef cubes in paper bag of seasoned flour, to coat them with flour. Remove mushrooms and onion, add more butter, and brown floured beef cubes in this. Stir in mushrooms, onion, 1 tablespoon tomato paste, and 4 tablespoons sour cream. Simmer 15 minutes and serve garnished with olives.

TWO: Pare and trim well all the fat and nerves from a nice tenderloin. Cut it lengthwise and en julienne, about 2 inches long and ½ inch thick. Put ¼ pound butter in a skillet and when very hot add the tenderloin strips. Cook over a quick fire and season with salt and pepper. Now add some finely chopped onions and minced mushrooms. When the moisture has evaporated from the mushrooms, wet them with thick sour cream and heat for 10 minutes, but without boiling. Arrange beef on a hot dish; pour the sauce over.

THREE: Slice 2 pounds fillet of beef into very thin little bits and mix with salt, pepper, and a little flour. Chop an onion fine and fry it in a saucepan in 2½ tablespoons butter. Add the bits of meat, fry together, and add ¼ cup bouillon (canned will do), 1 tablespoon Worcestershire sauce, and 1 cup sour cream. Mix well and cook without boiling until deep yellow-brown. Meantime, cut 10 mushrooms in small pieces and fry them separately in butter. Stir mushrooms into meat at the last minute, put into deep dish, and sprinkle with a little chopped parsley.

ROAST PRIME RIBS OF BEEF

Choose a well-marbled cut, 2 or 3 ribs. Wipe with a clean damp cloth. Rub with seasoned flour and place fat-side up, so the bones form a rack, in an uncovered roaster. Roast at 300°F (no water in the pan!) for 15 minutes per pound (rare), 20 minutes per pound (medium), or 30 minutes per pound (well-done). Don't baste. The low temperature of the oven reduces shrinkage, practically guarantees a tender, juicy roast. Remove to hot platter, garnish with parsley, serve with a red Bordeaux.

To serve browned potatoes and carrots with the roast, peel and partly cook the vegetables in boiling water, then ring them around the roast for the last hour in the oven. Baste them with pan drippings at the start of their roasting period. Turn them over when the tops are brown.

MINCED BEEF CHIARELLO

From Le Coq Rouge, New York

For 4, dice 2 cloves garlic; slice 2 mushrooms; sauté until soft in 1 ounce olive oil. Dice 2 pounds filet mignon and add to the soft garlic and mushrooms. Stir in 2 ounces of dry sherry, season to taste, increase heat, and sauté for 15 minutes, stirring.

POT ROAST

Handle lean or muscular cuts of beef this way. The usual method is to rub the meat with seasoned flour, brown it all over in hot fat, then reduce the heat and pour just enough liquid (stock preferred over water) in the pan to cover the bottom about ½ inch in depth. Cover the pan and simmer very gently until the meat is tender—2 to 3 hours for, say, 3 to 5 pounds of prime or choice beef. Add vegetables (peeled and sliced) for the last half-hour or so. Remove meat and vegetables when tender; thicken the stock with a roux or simply with flour.

ROAST CHICKEN

Linton Hopkins | Restaurant Eugene | Atlanta

AFTER GRADUATING FROM cooking school, I thought I had roast chicken figured out. I would stuff the cavity and use my Boy Scout knot-tying skills to truss the bird into a perfect little package. I would even massage the skin with butter. And I did get a good "presentation" bird that way. But for the home cook who isn't working on a photo shoot—and these days, that means me—I've now got a simple, easy way to get a delicious bird with golden-brown crackling skin and moist meat. This is chicken stripped of its pretense, and it reminds us why we love roast chicken. You can do a lot with this chicken. Put a cut lemon in the cavity during the roasting, or just squeeze lemon over the meat before serving. If you like the flavor of herbs, stuff the bird with a few stems of rosemary before putting it in the oven. Even when the chicken renders a lot of fat, the cast-iron skillet will keep that fat from burning; halfway through the cooking you can add some cut carrots or potatoes (use a small, uniform dice to shorten and even out the cooking time), or you can remove the cooked chicken to rest, pour off about half the fat, and sauté some greens in what's left. The whole process is incredibly fast. I can rinse, dry, season, and get the bird in the oven, and by the time I help my kids with their homework, dinner's ready.

SERVES 2 OR 3

DIFFICULTY:

EASY	REASONABLE	WORTH THE EFFORT

one 3- to 3½-lb chicken (see Tip)

1 tbsp kosher salt

coarsely ground black pepper

- Place an oven rack in the lower third of the oven and preheat to 450°F.

- Rinse the chicken inside and out under cold running water. Using paper towels, dry the bird thoroughly inside and out. The chicken must be bone dry or it will steam rather than brown. Set it in a cast-iron skillet and generously season with the salt and pepper to taste. Place the skillet in the preheated oven and go about your business for about 45 minutes.

- Slit the underside of a thigh—the juices should run clear. The high heat turns the chicken a golden brown, and it's juicy as hell.

BRAISED CHICKEN THIGHS
in Tomatillo Sauce

Koren Grieveson | Avec | Chicago

ONE-POT COOKING IS EASY AND EFFICIENT —maximum results from minimum effort. It's also forgiving, free of the pressure to time everything vigilantly. And you can improvise ingredients without upsetting the balance of what's in the pot, because there's time to adjust the seasoning during the long cooking process. In this braise, you can use pork shoulder or chicken thighs—dark meat handles long, slow cooking better than breast meat. Rather than buying prepackaged chicken, get the thighs from your butcher, for typically larger, more uniform thighs with the skin intact. This is key. When you braise chicken, there's no intramuscular fat. So the fat from the skin must render out during the sear and lace flavor through the cooking liquid. Add beans and call it a chili, serve it over rice and call it a stew, or wrap the tender boneless meat in a corn tortilla and call it a badass taco.

SERVES 4

DIFFICULTY:

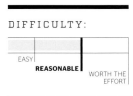

2 tbsp blended olive oil (see Note)

6 large chicken thighs, skin on and bone in (you can use skinless, but fat is flavor)

coarse salt and freshly ground black pepper

1 large carrot, peeled and chopped

2 stalks celery, sliced (reserve leaves for garnish)

1 white onion, chopped

2 tbsp garlic, chopped

1 jalapeño chile, sliced into rings (remove seeds for less heat)

2 bay leaves

5 small (7-oz) cans Mexican salsa verde, or 4 cups pureed tomatillos

3 tbsp torn fresh cilantro leaves (reserve and chop stems)

3½ cups low-sodium chicken stock

- In a braising pot over high heat, bring the olive oil almost to smoking. Season the thighs with salt and pepper and put in the pot, skin-side down. Once the skin is browned, flip and add the carrot, celery, onion, garlic, jalapeño, and bay leaves. Cook until the vegetables begin to exude moisture and the garlic starts to color, 6 to 8 minutes. (Move the thighs around so the vegetables hit the cooking surface.) Add the salsa verde, chopped cilantro stems, and chicken stock. Raise the heat and bring to a boil, then lower heat to a simmer and cover. Occasionally skim the foam from the surface and taste the liquid for seasoning, until the chicken is cooked through to the bone and tender, about 1 hour.

- Ladle into bowls, sprinkle with the reserved celery leaves and cilantro, and serve with rice and corn tortillas, passing a good hot sauce on the side.

  NOTE: Blended oil, available at the supermarket, is a mix of an oil with a high smoking point, such as grapeseed or canola, and olive oil, for flavor, so you can cook at higher temperatures and retain the taste of olive oil.

FOUR TECHNIQUES EVERY MAN SHOULD KNOW

HOW TO GRIP A KNIFE

BY BRIAN BISTRONG

Executive Chef of Braeburn in New York City

A knife is like a hammer or any other tool: Holding it properly increases the probability that you'll use it correctly. Here's how to grasp three knives essential in every kitchen.

• CHEF'S KNIFE

Pinch the blade between the thumb and forefinger just ahead of the bolster (the spot where the blade meets the handle) like a claw; curl the other three fingers around the handle. With your hand supported by the top of the bolster, your wrist can move up and down with just the right amount of freedom needed to chop vegetables with control and accuracy.

• SLICER

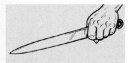

This knife, typically used for portioning and slicing protein, has a lighter, longer blade than a chef's knife. Grasp by wrapping all four fingers and the thumb around the handle, which allows you to use the knife in a more fluid motion with smooth strokes—as opposed to the rapid, staccatolike motion you use for chopping. Making small jerky motions can make a mess of the flesh on meat, fish, or poultry.

• PARING KNIFE

Just because this knife has a small blade doesn't mean you use it to chop small things like garlic cloves. It's typically used off the cutting board, with the blade pointing up, for precise work, such as trimming vegetables or peeling the skin from an onion or shallot. Grip the knife between thumb and index finger, down near the bolster for best control; hold the vegetable in the other hand, rotating it as you go.

HOW TO BRAISE

BY SHAWN McCLAIN

Chef and Owner of Spring and Custom House in Chicago

The art of braising meat begins with three simple principles: a tough cut of meat, a heavy-gauge pot, and a few cups of seasoned aromatic cooking liquid. Unlike poaching, braising uses low temperatures, less liquid, and a longer, slower cooking time so that connective tissue in the meat melts away, yielding moist, tender results. Since braising relies on the meat's own fat as a tenderizing agent, use less-expensive cuts of meat with more connective tissue—like chuck, brisket, or shoulder. Braising requires an ovenproof casserole pot heavy enough to regulate and distribute the heat evenly. Lids should fit tightly so the steam rises, collects, and condenses on the underside of the lid, then drips back into the pot. Meats are generally browned first. Blot the meat dry with paper towels (some recipes call for a light dusting of flour) and use just enough oil to lightly film the bottom of the pot and prevent the meat from sticking. (The meat should sizzle on contact, but the oil must not darken.) Sear on all sides, even the ends. Make sure you use a good base for your liquid, like quality store-bought natural stock. Wine-based braises are great too (add about ¼ or ½ cup to natural stock), especially when combined with aromatic vegetables and herbs. (After cooking vegetables have imparted their flavor to braising liquid, they are of little use and strained from the final sauce. Herbs as well; they lose their essential oils very quickly in cooking.) Once meat is browned and braising liquid added, bring to a simmer on top of the stove. This speeds up the process and reduces oven cooking time: Meat won't begin to tenderize until the braising liquid is around 180°F. (Although it can be done in the oven at a low temperature of about 300°F as well as on top of the stove, oven braising cooks meats more evenly without the vigilance required in the stove-top method.)

HOW TO SAUTÉ VEGETABLES

BY DAVID WALTUCK

Former Chef and Owner of Chanterelle in New York City

The French word *sauté* means "jump," and it comes from that fancy-looking move a chef makes when he moves a pan quickly back and forth across a burner to toss the food slightly up in the air. That's why the ideal sauté pan is flat with curved sides, ensuring that the food doesn't go flying all over the place when you flip it. Also, since all your food should touch the surface of the pan to ensure even cooking, you'll want a pan large enough to fit whatever you are cooking; never overcrowd. You only need a small amount of fat to sauté, and for vegetables, the best fat is olive oil—not something too pricey, just a good mid-range olive oil.

• FOR FIRM VEGETABLES:

Cut them into ½-inch cubes, the perfect size for uniform cooking; not too little to be a pain but still small enough to cook most vegetables through. Heat your pan until pretty darn hot but not smoking, then add 1 or 2 tablespoons olive oil. A few seconds later, add the vegetables. Don't play with your food and poke it around. Let it sit, soak up that fat, and then give it a couple of good tosses. Sautéing a vegetable, even a firm one, won't take very long, just a couple of min-

utes. It should come out of the pan a bit firm but not mushy. Add salt, pepper, some fresh chopped herbs, and a good squeeze of lemon; eat immediately.

• FOR LEAFY GREENS:

For greens like spinach, you can pretty much follow the same method as for firm vegetables, but you don't need to cut up the veggies, since leaves are fairly uniform in size. You do need to pay more attention, though. Greens cook quickly—just a quick toss or two will be enough to wilt them.

• SWEATING VERSUS SAUTÉING:

It's essentially a matter of heat level. Sweating happens over low heat and sautéing happens over high. Because the heat is lower, this generally means more cooking time overall, so the vegetables release their juices (or "sweat") but never brown. For example, it is common to sweat onions or shallots so that they soften and mellow.

HOW TO SEAR

BY CHARLIE PALMER

Chef and Owner of Charlie Palmer Restaurant Group

For years chefs talked about searing meat to caramelize the surface, forming a crust that seals in juices. Then a food-science writer named Harold McGee explained that the browning of meat isn't caramelization (which occurs only when sugar is present) at all. Still, though searing may not technically seal in juiciness, the contrast between the crust and the tender interior is otherworldly.

THE TOOLS:

• A heavy, thick-bottomed pan (like cast iron), which will evenly distribute heat and won't cool down when meat is added.

• Tongs. Stabbing with a fork will release all those precious juices. Just stab yourself with a fork and see what happens.

• Grapeseed oil, for its high smoking point. When oil smokes, it develops an acrid taste. Canola works fine too, and is cheaper. (Rule of thumb: The less flavor an oil has, the higher the smoking point.)

STEP 1: Warm the pan over high heat and add just enough oil to coat the bottom. Heat until the oil begins to "roll," moving in ripples when the pan is slightly shaken.

STEP 2: Dry the meat with a paper towel. Season well, showering salt over it from about a foot above, through your fingers. Pepper, too. Do this just before searing—if the salt draws out moisture, the resulting steam can inhibit browning.

STEP 3: Add the steaks, but leave about an inch between them, so any moisture evaporates immediately.

STEP 4: Reduce the heat to medium when you see that the edges of the meat touching the pan have browned (about 3 minutes). The sear is there; now we're going for some crust. Add extra oil if the pan is dry—most of the stuff you added in the beginning will now be spattered all over your stove top. Flip the steaks after 4 more minutes and sear the other side for 3 minutes. For more well-done, transfer pan to a 350°F oven to finish, 4 to 6 minutes. Remove the steaks from the pan and let rest for a good 5 minutes before serving. The juices need to redistribute themselves back into the meat before slicing.

ROASTED CHICKEN
with Red-Hot Rapini

Jimmy Bradley | The Red Cat | New York City

I'VE ALWAYS BELIEVED THAT roasted chicken is one of the barometers of a restaurant—a way to tell if the kitchen has a good grip on the fundamentals. A great chicken means that whoever's in the kitchen has laid a solid foundation for the rest of the menu, and that's what we did at the Red Cat. But sometimes, I'm still surprised by the number of people who want to talk to me about our chicken. And they all ask the same thing: What's the secret? It's kind of funny, because most people expect there to be some sort of "science" involved—some complicated process involving string and weights. But other than buying boneless halved chickens, the recipe couldn't be simpler. Although the method is similar to Cuban *pollo a la plancha* or Italian *pollo al mattone* (akin to American "chicken cooked under a brick"), we don't have to weight the breast down to make sure that all the skin is exposed to the heat. We do it all by boning the chicken half; it automatically lies flat against the pan. Then we crank the oven up, and the heat finds a way into every nook and cranny of the skin. No strings, no trussing, no bones—just a hot pan and a really hot oven. The result is crisp, crackly skin over moist, tender meat.

SERVES 4

DIFFICULTY:

EASY | REASONABLE | WORTH THE EFFORT

FOR CHICKEN

4 tbsp canola oil

two 3-lb chickens, halved and boned, skin on (see Tip)

coarse salt and freshly ground black pepper

- TO MAKE THE CHICKEN: Preheat the oven to 450°F.

- Heat 2 wide, deep, heavy-bottomed ovenproof skillets (cast-iron or a sturdy stainless steel pan, like All-Clad) over high heat. Put a small drop of water in each pan, and when it evaporates, it's time for the oil. Add 2 tablespoons canola oil to each pan and get it nice and hot. Place the chicken in the pans, skin-side down, making sure each piece lies flat and all skin is in contact with oil. Cook until skin is golden, 3 to 5 minutes. Transfer the pans to the oven and roast until the juices from the thickest part of both white and dark meat run clear when pierced by sharp, thin-bladed knife, about 20 minutes. Target meat temperature: 175°F.

TIP: Get your butcher to bone the bird, and buy grass-fed, pastured, or organic chicken; you will taste the difference.

TIP: Be specific with the butcher. Request a boneless chicken half, meaning that the first joint of the wing is clipped off and the only bone in the bird is the bone that attaches the lower part of the wing to the breast. Or use 2½ pounds boneless, skin-on chicken parts.

FOR RAPINI

2 tbsp olive oil, plus more for drizzling

1 tbsp canola oil

4 cloves garlic, thinly sliced

2 shallots, finely diced

2 bunches rapini (broccoli rabe; about 2 lb), bottom ½ inch trimmed off

¼ cup low-sodium chicken broth or water

coarse salt and freshly ground black pepper

generous pinch of crushed red pepper flakes

2 tbsp salted butter

1 lemon, halved

- TO MAKE THE RAPINI: Pour 1 tablespoon each of olive oil and canola oil into deep-sided sauté pan with a cover and place over medium heat. Add the garlic and shallots and sauté until light golden, about 3 minutes. Add the rapini, tossing to coat; add the broth and stir.

- Lower the heat, cover, and cook until the liquid is almost gone and the rapini is crisp-tender, about 8 minutes. Remove the cover and season with salt, pepper, and red pepper flakes. Stir in the butter and the remaining 1 tablespoon olive oil and toss to coat.

- TO SERVE: Top the rapini with a squeeze of lemon and a drizzle of olive oil. Lay over the chicken.

NOTE: Like spinach, rapini fills up the pan going in, shrinking as it cooks.

Spice-Rubbed
CHICKEN

Zakary Pelaccio | Fatty Crab | New York City

I LIVED IN MALAYSIA for a year, and this recipe grew out of the hawker stalls of Kuala Lumpur, where I first saw a woman cooking chicken sealed in waxed-paper bundles, in a wok layered with salt for slow, even cooking. The chicken had a pale, tender skin infused with herbs. The texture was addictive. That's why I don't brown the chicken in this adaptation. I don't want the skin to seize up. The result is a single-pot braise perfect for cold weather.

SERVES 2

DIFFICULTY:

EASY | **REASONABLE** | WORTH THE EFFORT

3 Thai chiles (thin-skinned hot red bird's-eye chiles) or fresh cayenne chiles, tops removed

½ inch young ginger (with green root and pink tips) or regular ginger

3 cloves garlic

2 fresh cilantro stems, leaves reserved

1 tsp ground turmeric

1 tbsp grated lime zest

one 3-lb fryer chicken, cut into 6 pieces

coarse salt and freshly ground black pepper

6 tbsp unsalted butter

2 medium white onions, cut into ½-inch rounds

3 stalks Chinese celery, or 4 thin interior stalks regular celery, cut into 2-inch pieces, leaves reserved

leaves from 2 sprigs fresh Vietnamese mint or regular mint, torn into small pieces

leaves from 2 sprigs Thai basil or Italian basil, torn

- Preheat the oven to 325°F. Using a food processor or blender (or mortar and pestle), grind the chiles, ginger, garlic, cilantro stems, turmeric, and lime zest into a paste. (It does not need to be completely smooth; avoid mixing until watery.)

- Rinse and dry the chicken very well. Season liberally with salt and pepper. In a bowl, use your hands to mash the butter until it softens; mix in spice paste. (If the butter starts to melt or becomes too soft, place in the refrigerator for about 15 minutes.) Rub the butter paste over the chicken pieces, coating all sides.

- Put the onions and celery in a heavy-duty pot (at least 5 quarts) and toss with salt and pepper. Arrange the chicken on the seasoned vegetables, cover the pot, and bake until the chicken breasts are cooked through but still moist, about 1½ hours, basting occasionally. Remove the breasts (spooning some cooking broth over them) and set aside, leaving the pot in the oven until the dark meat is thoroughly cooked, about another 15 minutes. Remove the pot from the oven, return the breasts, and let the dish rest, covered, for 15 to 20 minutes.

- In two shallow bowls, make a bed of vegetables and arrange chicken on top. Spoon liquid over; sprinkle with mint, basil, and cilantro leaves.

ESQUIRE
Classics

PRETTY EASY RECIPES FOR SOME OF THE BEST CHICKEN DISHES OF ALL TIME.

Reprinted from the *Esquire Cookbook*, 1955

ARROZ CON POLLO

Chicken with rice in the Spanish style

Season a disjointed chicken with salt and pepper and marinate it in lime juice for 1 1/2 hours. Sauté chicken in butter until golden brown and tender—30 to 40 minutes, probably. Meantime, make steamed rice to serve with the chicken and this sauce to pour over: Heat together 1/3 cup sherry, 1/4 pound quartered dates, a pinch of saffron, and 1 tablespoon shredded Canton or regular ginger. Put chicken on hot platter, with sauce on top and rice around. Garnish with watercress and thin slices of papaya.

CHICKEN IN THE POT

...With Noodles and Sour Cream

Best done in an old-fashioned bean pot. First, in a skillet, melt 2 tablespoons butter or fat, add 2 cloves minced garlic, and brown in this a jointed chicken. (Figure 3/4 to 1 pound per serving.) Add 1 chopped onion or leek, 1 minced green pepper, 3 stalks chopped celery, 1/4 cup chopped ripe olives. When they are lightly browned, add 1 1/2 cups Marsala wine and a pinch each of oregano, thyme, salt, and cayenne. Put into a bean pot and cover the chicken with hot water. Clamp on the lid, place in a medium oven, and cook until the chicken is tender—around 2 hours for a mature bird. Add a pound package of noodles and step up the heat for 15 more minutes. Remove, stir in 1 pint sour cream, adjust seasoning and rush to the table. Good accompaniments: watercress in a tart French dressing, a toasted loaf of Italian bread, and the balance of the Marsala wine.

CHICKEN ROMANA

From Theodore's, New York

For 2 hungry or polite people, quarter a 2- to 2 1/2-pound chicken and shake the pieces in a paper bag of salt-and-peppered flour. Melt 2 tablespoons butter in 1/2 cup olive oil. Sauté the chicken in this until lightly browned. Add 1/2 minced garlic clove, 1 tablespoon rosemary, and 1 1/2 teaspoons salt; continue sautéing until golden brown. Add 1 tablespoon wine vinegar and 1/2 cup chicken broth (made from giblets or bouillon cubes). Place in a casserole and bake in a moderate oven until ready to serve—about 20 minutes. Perfection with a bottle of cold white wine.

CHICKEN PAPRIKASCH

The only true way to make this Hungarian dish, according to gourmet-Hungarian Iles Brody, who wrote in *Esquire*: "I put my foot down on this question and dogmatically assert that most cookbooks and most chefs in this country are wrong about chicken paprikasch." Here is the real goods:

Allow 2 cut-up spring chickens for 4 persons. Chop 3 large onions up fine, put in a heavy pan with a tablespoon of lard, and cook very, very gently over a very slow fire for almost an hour, until it becomes almost a jelly. Be sure that it does not burn. Add 1 tablespoon paprika; let the paprika and the jelly simmer another 10 minutes. Now put in the cut-up chicken and let it stew, well covered, for a half-hour. Put in 2 green peppers, all cut up, and salt to taste. Let it stew another half hour, then mix in 1 teaspoon flour and 2 tablespoons sweet cream. Boil it for a split second; if you boil it longer it will become watery. Serve with dumplings or boiled rice.

Coca-Cola-Brined

FRIED CHICKEN

John Currence | City Grocery | Oxford, Mississippi

AFTER KATRINA, I HELPED rebuild the fifty-year-old Willie Mae's Scotch House, one of the city's culinary landmarks. This is my attempt at re-creating Willie Mae's secret-recipe chicken, the best I've ever eaten. The Coca-Cola gives it a sweetness that plays nicely against the cayenne. I added pickle-garlic relish as a nod to the late, great Austin Leslie, another New Orleans cook and a high priest of the deep-fat chicken fryer. He died after evacuating his home after the storm. This dish is a tip of the hat to two of the best I've had the pleasure of knowing.

SERVES 4

DIFFICULTY:

EASY · REASONABLE · **WORTH THE EXTRA EFFORT**

BRINING CHICKEN

12 chicken thighs, bone-in, skin-on

4 cups **Coca-Cola**

1 tsp liquid smoke (optional)

2½ tbsp Worcestershire sauce

1 tbsp **Tabasco** sauce

3 tbsp coarse salt

3 tbsp freshly ground black pepper

BATTER

1 large egg

¾ cup peanut oil

2 tsp baking powder

2 tbsp coarse salt

4 tsp freshly ground black pepper

1 tbsp cayenne pepper

1 tbsp onion powder

1 tbsp garlic powder

2½ cups all-purpose flour

FRYING CHICKEN

peanut oil and lard

coarse salt and freshly ground black pepper

PICKLE-GARLIC RELISH

1 cup fresh flat-leaf parsley

1 cup dill-pickle chips, plus a little pickle juice if desired

3 tbsp minced garlic

CONTINUED

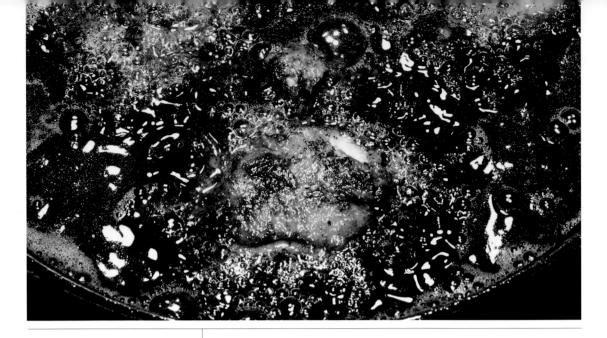

- **TO BRINE THE CHICKEN:** Rinse the chicken, drain, and set aside. Combine all the remaining brining ingredients in a large bowl, stirring until the salt dissolves. Put the chicken in the brine, cover, and marinate, refrigerated, for 4 hours.

- **TO MAKE THE BATTER:** Whisk the egg well in a stainless steel bowl and add the peanut oil and 2½ cups water. In a separate bowl, combine all the remaining batter ingredients, then add the dry mixture to the egg mixture, whisking slowly so the batter doesn't clump.

- **TO FRY THE CHICKEN:** Fill a large cast-iron skillet halfway with equal amounts of peanut oil and lard. Slowly bring the temperature to 375°F. (Use a deep-fat thermometer.)

- While the oil is heating, remove the chicken from the brine and place in a colander in the sink. Once the chicken has drained, pat it dry with paper towels (a critical step) and season with salt and pepper. Dip the chicken in the batter and place it (carefully) in the hot oil. Adjust the heat, as the chicken will bring the oil temperature down dramatically—you want it back up to just above 350°F. Turn the chicken regularly using tongs to prevent burning. After 8 or 9 minutes, remove a piece, prick it to the bone with a fork, and mash it. If the juices run clear, it's done. Continue cooking if necessary.

- **TO MAKE THE PICKLE-GARLIC RELISH:** Finely chop and combine all the relish ingredients.

- Serve with the chicken. Cover any leftovers with a dish towel and leave out at room temperature (or in the fridge, if you must, although my grandmother never did). This keeps it crisp.

Makes about 1 ½ cups.

CONTINUED FROM

EATING WITH MY FATHER

WE HAD A LOT OF TOUGH TALKS. FOR SOME REASON,
THEY WERE ALWAYS EASIER OVER LUNCH.

By Tom Chiarella

AROUND THE HOUSE, my dad was a brooding, intense guy. He glared. He shouted. At the end of a workday, standing at his roll-top desk, holding a sheaf of bills, looking over his shoulder at some disturbance in the living room, he flat-out scared me. But I loved eating with my dad. I would tell him anything when we ate. The guy was clear-eyed and wise over a bowl of soup.

During high school, we ate every Saturday at a restaurant high atop an office tower in Rochester, New York. I had to get there first, pick a booth by a north-facing window, leave room for him to sit on the left, and order two Tabs with lemon. Every major conversation I had with the guy during those years occurred in that booth, over lunch. I had quit football suddenly. I'd banged up the car. I'd been in a fight. I'd cashed out my savings bonds without telling him. I'd paid for a girlfriend's abortion. Through all this we ate. In this way, we got through it. Food filled the silences. Onion soup. Escarole and beans. New potatoes flecked with skin. Spinach—always spinach. T-bones. Hard rolls. French fries with grilled onions. Over time, my father told me his share, too: that he'd been married once before, that his new boss had refused to pay him for nearly a year, that his business seemed to be at an end. At these times, I could see that he was eating with a purpose: He ate like he meant it.

He had his quirks—he liked lemon wedges with his salad, he ate the tails of cooked shrimp, he despised the way I used butter—but he was not overly concerned with the rituals or compulsions of food. When he allowed himself to gravitate toward the comfort foods of an immigrant's childhood—tripe, chicken gizzards, even bone mar-row—he amazed me. A proffered forkful of food from my dad was his way of teaching. He wanted me to try things, to open myself up beyond cheeseburgers and tuna melts.

And I gave it a shot, because there in that booth with the food in front of us, my dad could be trusted. When we were eating, I discovered him to be more than what I thought he was: braver, tougher, more generous, and more exotic than anyone I knew. When he ate, I wanted to be him.

I'm almost fifty now. The last time I ate with my dad, he was living in a nursing home outside Albany. We'd sat in a big room, fluorescents and linoleum, full of skeletons four to a table eating tapioca out of paper cups. He was still brave about the food, although for different reasons. It was a struggle just to eat, for one thing—he did the best he could with a fork, and I fed him the rest. And the food wasn't that good, of course, though he seemed to like the cheesecake. Despite how it sounds, none of this was particularly sad, except that now he didn't talk while he ate. He couldn't. I tried talking for a while, but I could see it stressed him. So then I was quiet. Yes, that part was sad. My father had forgotten what food was for—what he and I used it for—and that was unbearable. Eventually, though, he looked up and said, "You would like the cheesecake." I nodded and went to get a piece, offered him some off my own fork, but he didn't want any more. He said, "Go on, try it." And he was right. It was good cheesecake, better than I thought it would be. It was delicious.

"You look good when you eat," my dad said. It was something he said sometimes.

"You eat like you mean it."

PESCE
alla Palermitana

Paul Bartolotta | Bartolotta Ristorante di Mare | Las Vegas

EVERY LITTLE AREA OF Italy has its own culinary style—there's a lot more to it than Tuscany. I first had *pesce alla palermitana* ("Palermo-style fish") in Sicily in 1978 and was so blown away by the flavors of the sauce that, though I never actually made the dish until this year, I had them logged away in my memory. This dish is traditionally made with a whole fish baked in the oven. I modified it, as I do all the time, by using filleted fish, most often orata (or sea bream, called *dorade royal* in France), a moist, delicate fish found at most quality markets. (Substitute another thin fillet fish, like red snapper, rather than a thick barrel fish like tuna.) The Sicilian kitchen has a strong undercurrent of other cuisines, mostly from Greece and the Arab world, and these are highlighted in the sauce, with capers—the most pungent are from Pantelleria, typically preserved with salt rather than brine—and meaty green olives like Cerignola, known for their bright color and young, slightly sweet taste. Simmering the lemon in its rind—almost Moroccan style—releases not only the juice but the mellow richness of the lemon's oil. What's most rewarding is that the flavor isn't "added"; it develops organically with the ingredients. It took me twenty years of trends and foams and emulsions to circle back, find this food, and have the courage to appreciate the elegance of such simplicity.

SERVES 2

DIFFICULTY:

4 oz fingerling potatoes (at least 3)

4 tbsp extra-virgin olive oil, plus more for drizzling

1 clove garlic, peeled and thinly sliced

10 oz cherry tomatoes (about 2 cups), quartered

8 green olives, pitted and sliced

2 tbsp capers, rinsed and drained

4 sprigs fresh oregano, plus 1 tbsp chopped

1 lemon, quartered

¼ cup dry white wine

two 6-oz orata (sea bream) fillets or red snapper or American bass fillets

coarse salt and freshly ground black pepper

1 tbsp chopped fresh flat-leaf parsley

- In a saucepan of cold water, bring the fingerlings to a boil and cook for 6 to 8 minutes. Drain, cut in half lengthwise, and set aside.

- Preheat the oven to 450°F. In a large (12-inch) ovenproof sauté pan over medium heat, warm 2 tablespoons of the olive oil. Add the garlic and cook until lightly browned, about 3 minutes. Add the tomatoes, potatoes, olives, capers, oregano sprigs, lemon, and white wine. Season the fish with salt and pepper and place skin-side up in the pan. Add ¼ cup water and bake in the oven for 8 minutes, or until the fish has reached an internal temperature of 140°F. Remove the fish from the pan and set aside.

- Place the pan over high heat and simmer until the liquid is reduced by half. Add the chopped oregano and parsley and the remaining 2 tablespoons olive oil. Adjust the seasoning. Divide the sauce evenly (including the potatoes and lemon wedges) between two plates. Place the fish on top of the sauce and drizzle with olive oil.

OYSTER STEW

Scott Peacock | Chef, cookbook author

DRIVE SIXTY MILES FROM my hometown in Alabama and you come to the Gulf of Mexico. During our cold-weather months, there were temporary shacks that served up Apalachicolas. They'd shuck 'em for you until you told them to stop. It was a social thing to do, mostly involving the men in town. Our oyster stew was also the domain of men, with recipes passed down from father to son. The first bowl I ever tasted came via a friend of my father's—the only thing he knew how to make, the only time he went into the kitchen.

SERVES 4

DIFFICULTY:

5 tbsp unsalted butter, plus softened butter for bread

1 yellow onion, diced (about 1 cup)

1 tsp coarse salt, plus more to taste

2 tbsp all-purpose flour

3 cups milk, warmed

1 cup heavy cream

2 to 3 dozen fresh stewing oysters, shucked and picked over to remove any shells, liquor strained and reserved (about 1 cup)

freshly ground black pepper

pinch of ground cayenne

4 slices good white bread

- In a nonreactive saucepan (stainless, 4-quart) over medium-low heat, melt 3 tablespoons of the butter. Add the onion and salt; stir well to coat. Cook slowly, stirring often, until the onion is tender but not browned, about 10 minutes. Sprinkle the flour over the onion, stirring well to blend, and cook 2 minutes longer. Slowly whisk in the heated milk and heavy cream, along with the reserved oyster liquor. Bring just to a light simmer, stirring often to prevent scorching.

- In a wide nonstick skillet over medium-high heat, melt the remaining 2 tablespoons of butter until hot and bubbling but not browned. Add the drained oysters in a single layer. Sprinkle with coarse salt and black pepper; sauté until the oysters begin to curl on the edges and the gills are slightly exposed, about 2 minutes. Do not overcook.

- Transfer the entire contents of the oyster sauté pan to the onion-milk mixture. Stir in a pinch of cayenne, cover, and remove from heat to "ripen" for 10 minutes, allowing the flavors to develop.

- Spread the softened butter on the bread and serve with the stew.

Bourbon and Brown-Sugar

SALMON

Mark Gaier and Clark Frasier |
Arrows and MC Perkins Cove | Ogunquit, Maine

SERVES 2

DIFFICULTY:

EASY | REASONABLE | WORTH THE EFFORT

2 pieces salmon fillet (1½ inches thick)

coarse salt and freshly ground black pepper

2 tbsp butter

¼ cup packed brown sugar

¼ cup bourbon

- Rinse the salmon fillets, pat dry, and season with salt and pepper.

- Heat a skillet over medium to high heat; when hot, add the butter and melt without burning. Once the foaming subsides, add the brown sugar and stir until combined. Add the salmon and cook for 3 to 4 minutes. Flip and add the bourbon; cook until the desired doneness, about 3 minutes.

Tandoori-Spiced

RED SNAPPER

Eric Ripert | Le Bernardin | New York City

INSTEAD OF STARTING with a recipe and then shopping with a list of ingredients, here's a thrilling way to cook: You buy what's freshest and then go home and figure out what to do with it. Try it. If you start to learn what to do with your unexpected purchase without looking up a recipe, your food will taste better—and you'll live forever, because your food will always be fresh. You usually just need a little basic knowledge, some confidence, and a few ingredients you probably already have.* With this page, you can add fish to your list of foods you know how to handle without thinking. The recipe is really more than a recipe. It's a simple, timeless lesson in the way fish responds to heat. It also happens to be a good way to get dinner on the table in about nine minutes.

SERVES 1

DIFFICULTY:

EASY | REASONABLE | WORTH THE EFFORT

½ tbsp butter, softened but not melted

one 6-oz skinless red snapper fillet, ¾ inch thick

fine sea salt and ground white pepper

1 tsp tandoori powder

2 tbsp extra-virgin olive oil

¼ cup freshly squeezed lemon juice

- Preheat the broiler. Cover the bottom of a baking sheet with aluminum foil and lightly brush an area a little bigger than the piece of fish with half of the softened butter.

- Season the fish on both sides with salt and pepper, holding your hand about 5 inches away to focus the seasonings. Liberally brush the top with the softened butter and season with some of the tandoori spice. Place the fish buttered-side up on the buttered baking sheet and broil for about 5 minutes, until the fish just starts to flake.

- While the fish is cooking, stir together the remaining tandoori spice, the olive oil, and lemon juice. Transfer the snapper fillet to a plate and drizzle the tandoori oil over and around the fish.

SUBSTITUTE: If your fish store is out of red snapper, you can try this recipe with another white fish. Striped bass, halibut, and branzino are all good options.

TIP: If you get a piece of fish that's thin on one end, you can just tuck the tail under to make it cook more evenly.

TIP: Is it done? Insert a thin metal skewer into the fish and then hold it against your chin. The skewer should feel warm. If it's too hot, the fish is overcooked and that's your punishment.

*Okay, you might not have tandoori powder, but it's available at good spice shops and high-end groceries. You could use herbes de Provence instead.

Seafood
HOT POT

Bryan Caswell | Reef | Houston

THIS IS A MELTING POT OF classic fisherman's stews: cioppino, bouillabaisse, gumbo, jambalaya, and paella—all opportunistic dishes born from the unpredictability of the day's catch. My whole life I've fished in camp houses up and down the Gulf Coast, and every day our focus is to catch that night's dinner. A dish like this works well no matter what fish you get—in the wild or at your seafood market. It's a one-pot dish that works year-round.

SERVES 4

DIFFICULTY:

| EASY | REASONABLE | WORTH THE EFFORT |

THE BASE

6 tbsp unsalted butter

3 tbsp tomato paste

MIX 1

½ head celery, minced

1 medium onion, finely chopped

1 small bulb fennel, diced

5 cloves garlic, minced

2 Thai (red) chiles, minced

MIX 2

1 tsp freshly ground black pepper

½ tsp cayenne pepper

1 tsp coarse salt

MIX 3

½ cup dry white wine

½ cup carrot juice

MIX 4

one 14.5-oz can whole tomatoes, drained

4 cups clam juice

2 cups chicken stock

large bunch fresh thyme, tied with kitchen twine

¾ lb fingerling potatoes, cut into ¼-inch-thick rounds

- TO MAKE THE BASE: In a large pot over medium heat, melt 4 of the tablespoons butter until foamy. Stir in Mixes 1 and 2, cooking until vegetables are translucent with slightly browned edges, 8 to 10 minutes. Halfway through the cooking process, add the remaining 2 tablespoons of butter. Lower the heat and stir in the tomato paste. Mix well and cook until the paste begins to brown (not burn), about 5 minutes.

- Add Mix 3 and stir to scrape up the browned bits on the bottom of the pot. Simmer to reduce by half, about 6 minutes.

- Stir in Mix 4 and raise the heat to a boil. Lower the heat and simmer until the potatoes are tender. Set aside and keep warm.

SEAFOOD

8 clams in shells, scrubbed

8 mussels in shells, scrubbed and debearded

8 medium shrimp, peeled and deveined

8 large sea scallops

8 oz skinless snapper or other white fish fillets

coarse salt

cayenne pepper

¼ cup olive oil

4 shallots, minced

1 cup dry vermouth

- Season the seafood with salt and cayenne. In a jumbo pasta pot or Dutch oven (wide cooking surface, high sides), heat the olive oil. Add the clams and mussels, sautéing for about 1½ minutes. Add the shrimp, scallops, fish, and shallots, cooking until the seafood is opaque on one side, about 1 minute. (Don't flip.) Add the vermouth, cover, and let the mixture steam until the seafood is cooked through, 90 seconds or so.

- Add the hot base and bring to a low boil, simmering 1½ minutes. Remove the thyme and discard.

SPAGHETTI CARBONARA

Frank Crispo | Crispo | New York City

BY THE TIME I WENT TO culinary school, I'd already come up through the kitchen ranks, working in Italian restaurants around Philly. But my dad was a plumber, so I also grew up with a wrench in my hand, learning how to fix things. Recipes are no different. You have to tinker with a dish until it works for you. In traditional *spaghetti alla carbonara*, egg yolk is added to the hot pasta and starts to cook on contact. Unless you're eating immediately, the *carbonara* becomes gluey. You can be engrossed in conversation, and by the time you're ready to take a bite, the whole bowl of pasta seems to come up with your fork. I use a poached egg on top of the pasta instead. The yolk is already warm when it hits the noodles, so they blend easier—it gives it richness without binding. I made a few other tweaks so the dish doesn't feel quite so heavy, like adding frisée lettuce for texture and sharp pecorino romano to balance the Parmigiano-Reggiano, which is buttery. But the heart of the dish is the three p's: pancetta, smoked pancetta (it's okay to substitute smoked bacon), and prosciutto di San Daniele. Unlike prosciutto from Parma, typically salted for four weeks, Daniele is salted for only three, leaving the ham moist and a little sweeter. In Italian, *carbone* translates as "coal." The story is that miners (who always had cured pork in their knapsacks) cooked it over open fires, and the charcoal would flake off and scatter across the pasta. I use coarsely ground black pepper instead.

SERVES 2

DIFFICULTY:

8 to 10 oz spaghetti

6 tbsp distilled white vinegar

2 oz thickly sliced pancetta, cut into 1/2-inch dice

2 oz thickly sliced smoked pancetta, or 2 slices smoked slab bacon, cut into 1/2-inch dice

2 oz thickly sliced prosciutto di San Daniele or prosciutto di Parma, cut into 1/2-inch dice

1 cup low-sodium chicken broth

1 cup chopped frisée lettuce

3 tbsp chopped fresh flat-leaf parsley

coarse salt and coarsely ground black pepper

1 tbsp unsalted butter

2 tbsp extra-virgin olive oil

1/3 cup grated Parmigiano-Reggiano

1/3 cup grated pecorino romano, preferably Locatelli

2 extra-large eggs

- In a gallon of abundantly salted boiling water, cook the pasta until al dente, 8 to 10 minutes. Drain but do not rinse.

- Bring a sauté pan of water to a boil and leave on low heat; add the vinegar.

- In large (12-inch) sauté pan over medium-low heat, cook the diced pork until the fat renders and the meat is slightly crisp, about 10 minutes. Add the broth and simmer to reduce by one-third, 8 to 10 minutes. Add the lettuce, parsley, salt, and pepper. Add the drained pasta, raise the heat to high, and toss to coat with the sauce. Add the butter and olive oil and toss until the pasta is well coated. Turn off the heat, sprinkle in the cheese, and toss. Divide the pasta between two warm serving bowls.

- Working one at a time, carefully crack each egg into a small bowl and very gently slide into the barely boiling water liquid. Cook until the whites set but the yolks are still runny, about 2 minutes. Using a slotted spoon, lift each egg out of the water. After you lift the egg, touch the back of the slotted spoon to a kitchen towel to remove excess water clinging to the bottom. Place an egg atop each bowl of pasta. Add a generous grind of black pepper. Eat immediately, mixing up the pasta to spread the egg and yolk throughout the bowl.

LAMB RAGÙ

with Pistachios and Mint

Emma Hearst | Sorella | New York City

WHEN IT COMES TO FEEDING MEN —or anyone who knows how to eat— you have to respect the meat-and-potatoes appetite, even when the meal isn't exactly meat. Or potatoes. I put this sauce together out of things I had on hand: part luck, part learning. It's a traditional Bolognese sauce right up to the moment you drop in the orange. Juice alone wouldn't have enough citrus power to cut through the richness of the lamb—it's the essential oils from the rind that create a sweet undercurrent in the sauce. When you have a sauce this rich and complex, you want a flat noodle that provides some surface cling. A round noodle won't grip the sauce, and the best part of the meal will slip away.

SERVES 6

DIFFICULTY:

EASY | **REASONABLE** | WORTH THE EFFORT

½ lb pancetta, finely diced

extra-virgin olive oil

1 yellow onion, finely diced

2 carrots, finely diced

2 stalks celery, finely diced

2 cloves garlic, minced

2 lb ground lamb

6 oz tomato paste

1 cup dry white wine

1 cup whole milk

3 tbsp fennel seeds

2 tbsp ground cardamom

1 orange, quartered

coarse salt

1 cup coarsely chopped mint leaves

1½ cups roughly chopped unsalted pistachios (from about 3 cups in shell)

2 lb thin hand-cut fresh long pasta, such as tagliarini or tagliatelle

2 tbsp unsalted butter

1½ cups ricotta cheese

1 tbsp freshly ground black pepper

• In a large pot over medium heat, render the pancetta slightly with a drizzle of extra-virgin olive oil. (Do not brown.) When the pancetta is translucent, about 8 minutes, add the onion, carrots, celery, and garlic. Lower the heat and cook until the vegetables are translucent and soft, about 12 minutes. (Do not brown.) Add the lamb and cook, working it with a wooden spoon so all the meat touches the cooking surface, until it loses its pink color, about 12 minutes. Add the tomato paste and cook, stirring frequently, until it turns rust colored, 3 to 5 minutes. Add up to ½ cup water and stir to loosen tomato paste so it doesn't burn. Add the wine and simmer for 2 minutes, stirring to scrape up the browned bits from the bottom of the pot. Add the milk, fennel seeds, cardamom, orange, and 1 tablespoon salt.

Stir to combine. Cover and barely simmer over extremely low heat until the flavors are thoroughly blended, about 1½ hours. (Use the lowest possible heat source to avoid scorching, and stir frequently to avoid sticking.)

- Skim off the fat and discard, remove and discard the orange, and season with salt to taste. Stir in the mint and pistachios and add about ½ cup to 1 cup water to thin the ragù slightly.

- Cook the pasta in salted boiling water according to package directions, but when the noodles are about 1 minute from al dente (still a little sticky to the touch), transfer them to the sauce to finish cooking. Add the butter and reduce until the sauce clings to the pasta. Use tongs to toss the noodles in the sauce. Salt to taste. Stir the ricotta and pepper together and serve with the pasta.

SPAGHETTI
all'Amatriciana

Marco Canora | Terroir | New York City

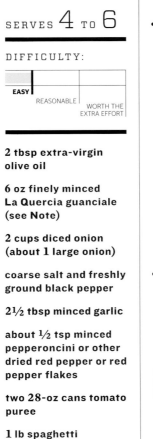

SERVES 4 TO 6

DIFFICULTY:

| **EASY** | REASONABLE | WORTH THE EXTRA EFFORT |

2 tbsp extra-virgin olive oil

6 oz finely minced La Quercia guanciale (see Note)

2 cups diced onion (about 1 large onion)

coarse salt and freshly ground black pepper

2½ tbsp minced garlic

about ½ tsp minced pepperoncini or other dried red pepper or red pepper flakes

two 28-oz cans tomato puree

1 lb spaghetti

• Heat the oil in a large pot over medium heat until the oil ripples but does not smoke. Add the guanciale and cook, stirring frequently, until the fat begins to render and the meat is no longer pink, about 3 minutes. Add the onion and stir, coating with the rendered fat. Season with salt and pepper and cook, stirring occasionally, until the onions are soft and golden, about 10 minutes. Add the garlic and pepperoncini and cook, stirring occasionally, until the mixture is aromatic, about 10 minutes more. Add the tomato puree, season with salt and pepper, and bring to a boil. Lower the heat and gently simmer the sauce, stirring occasionally, until it reduces and thickens slightly, the flavors blend, and the fat floats to the surface, about 40 minutes.

• At this point the sauce can be used immediately, or cooled and refrigerated for up to a week, or cooled and frozen. If using immediately: In a large pot of salted boiling water, cook the spaghetti until al dente. Drain but don't rinse, return the spaghetti to the hot pot, and toss with the sauce.

NOTE: We highly recommend La Quercia—its earthy, porky goodness is hard to beat—but other brands will work.

CAVATELLI

with Wilted Greens, Crispy Pancetta, and Chickpeas

Scott Conant | Scarpetta | New York City

SERVES 4 TO 6

DIFFICULTY:

EASY | REASONABLE | WORTH THE EFFORT

2 tbsp extra-virgin olive oil

4 oz pancetta, diced

2 medium shallots, thinly sliced

one 15-oz can chickpeas (about 1⅔ cups), drained

1 small bunch mustard greens or other bitter greens, trimmed of tough stems, well washed, and coarsely chopped (about 2 cups)

coarse salt

1 lb fresh or frozen cavatelli pasta

¼ cup grated Parmigiano-Reggiano cheese, or more to taste

- Bring a large pot of well-salted water to a boil.

- Heat 1 tablespoon of the olive oil in a large sauté pan over medium-high heat. Add the pancetta and cook, stirring occasionally, until crisp. Remove the pancetta with a slotted spoon (but don't clean the pan) and set aside. Add the remaining 1 tablespoon oil to the pan and heat over medium heat. Add the shallots and cook, stirring occasionally, until tender. Add the chickpeas and the greens, season lightly with salt, and cook until the greens have wilted, about 3 minutes.

- Meanwhile, cook the cavatelli in the boiling water until just shy of al dente. Reserve about 1 cup of the cooking water, then drain the pasta. Add the pasta, pancetta, and ½ cup of the pasta water to the chickpeas and greens. Cook, adding more pasta water if the mixture looks dry, until the pasta is al dente. Add the Parmigiano and toss again. Serve.

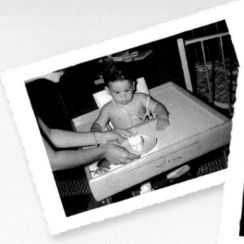

A BRIEF BIOGRAPHY,
IN FOOD

By Mike Sager

WHEN I WAS YOUNG, I wore "husky"-sized corduroys. I remember walking through the shopping center, my thighs rubbing together made a noise. We'd see an obese person and my mother would warn: "You, too, could look like that."

Once, at the Suburban House, a kosher deli in Baltimore, my father and grandfather wrestled for the check. My grandfather was seated at the head of the table; he never let my father pay for dinner. My father, who was probably in his late thirties at the time, came around behind him and tried to pry the vinyl portfolio out of his hands. I think my father's feet went off the ground at some point. When the portfolio tore in half, my father gave up the battle.

For many years, this was my diet: Breakfast: coffee and two cigarettes. Midmorning snack: coffee and more cigarettes. Lunch: a chocolate-chip cookie (or a package of peanut-butter crackers), more coffee, more cigarettes. Afternoon snack: coffee and cigarettes. After work, I hit the gym.

I spent a few months, off and on, doing maneuvers with the U.S. Marines. I subsisted as the troops did, on MREs. Every morning at the crack of dawn, I would walk a little distance from camp and crouch behind a rock or a bush. Usually there were other dim shapes scattered around me; that's how they roll in the Marines. The second night I was home, I went out to dinner at a fancy restaurant with my wife and some friends. There was much lively discussion about which wine to order. Everyone weighed in with their up-to-date and erudite opinions. All I could think about was how good it had felt that morning to sit on a real toilet, alone, and take a shit.

Now that I am in my fifties, my father never lets me pay for dinner, either. Sometimes I outsmart him by giving my credit card to the maître d' in advance.

SPAGHETTI

with Lobster, Chiles, and Mint

Dave Pasternack | Esca | New York City

I'VE BEEN A FISHERMAN MY whole life—started with my father when I was about five, in Jamaica Bay, Brooklyn, and I still catch some of what's served at Esca. But I also get everything from everywhere: Alaskan salmon, abalone from British Columbia, John Dory from New Zealand. I don't have a preconceived notion of what I'm going to do with each fish; the preparation and ingredients are based on the state the fish is in—the seasonal differences, which affect fishing just as much as farming. Take lobster: People like it in the summer, but it's actually better during the winter, when colder water and harder shells mean more meat for your money. In this dish, I take the small one-pounders, called "chicks," and turn them into a bigger meal. Like all peasant-style cooking, this dish ekes the most out of every expensive ingredient, like draining the cooking water from the lobster claws to add to the sauce and sautéing the tails in the shells to pull out every ounce of flavor. I've had this dish on my menu since I opened the restaurant. It'll get you a lot of love for very little cooking time.

SERVES 4

DIFFICULTY:

coarse salt

four 1-lb live lobsters
(see **Tips**)

1 lb spaghetti

4 tbsp olive oil

2 cloves garlic, peeled and sliced paper-thin

4 fresh hot chiles (poblano, habanero, Holland, serrano), diced
(about ¼ cup)
(see **Note**)

2 cups good tomato sauce

freshly ground black pepper

10 fresh mint leaves, chiffonade (cut into thin strips on the diagonal)

- Bring a pot of water to a boil and add salt until it tastes like seawater. Set the lobster tails aside and cook the claws in the salted water for 5 minutes. Remove and crack open using the back of a knife. Reserve any interior water and juices from the shells and add it to the final sauce for flavor boost.

- Bring another pot of abundantly salted water to a boil, add the spaghetti, and cook until al dente, about 8 minutes. Drain but do not rinse, reserving 1 cup cooking water.

- Cut each tail in half lengthwise and then widthwise, yielding 4 pieces.

- Heat 3 tablespoons of the oil in large sauté pan over medium heat and add the tail pieces (the shell still attached to the meat). When the lobster meat begins to look white (about 2 minutes), add the garlic and chiles and cook until softened, 3 to 5 minutes. Add the reserved pasta water, tomato sauce, and cooked lobster claws and simmer, reducing the sauce to thicken, about 5 minutes. Add the pasta to the sauce, tossing to coat. Add the remaining 1 tablespoon oil and any reserved liquid from the claws; season with salt and pepper to taste. Divide the pasta among 4 warmed serving bowls and sprinkle with mint.

TIP: If you buy the lobsters within a few hours of when you're going to use them, have the fishmonger do the dirty work: Ask him to separate the claws, split the tails into four pieces, and discard the bodies.

TIP: Cracking the lobster claws with the back of a knife is messy. Here's our solution: Place the claws in a deep bowl to prevent splattering and use a lobster cracker. Added bonus: The cooking water from the claws stays right in the bowl.

NOTE: The more seeds you leave in the peppers, the hotter the dish will be.

Ratatouille

RISOTTO

Sean Brock | McCrady's | Charleston, South Carolina

RICE ONCE RULED the river marshes outside colonial Charleston, and risotto is kin to our traditional low-country pilau. Although I often use heritage Carolina Gold grain, classic risotto is made with Arborio rice, originally found in Italy's Po Valley but now grown in Texas. Arborio is a stubby, milky grain that heat-releases amylopectin, a starch that gives risotto its creamy but chewy texture. Charleston's historic influence also shows up in the Spanish-tinged sofrito, a mixture of aromatics cooked so slowly, it almost melts away. And because we're at the height of summer's produce season, I load in ratatouille-style vegetables from my own farm. Your local green market should be just as plentiful. Remember that freshly picked vegetables have a shiny exterior, and that squash and eggplant should feel "tight" (squishy = loaded with water = soggy). Once you get the technique down, stop short of adding the tomatoes and create your own variation. This is just your gateway recipe.

SERVES 4

DIFFICULTY:

EASY | **REASONABLE** | WORTH THE EFFORT

RATATOUILLE

1½ cups diced bell peppers

1½ cups diced Japanese eggplant

1½ cups diced zucchini

1½ cups diced yellow squash

1 tbsp balsamic vinegar

3 tbsp olive oil

3 torn fresh basil leaves

fresh thyme leaves

2 tbsp chopped fresh flat-leaf parsley

- TO MAKE THE RATATOUILLE: Preheat the oven to 450°F. Combine the peppers (whatever color), eggplant, zucchini, and squash in a bowl. Add the balsamic vinegar, olive oil, a few basil leaves torn into pieces, leaves from a few sprigs of fresh thyme, and parsley. Toss to coat and spread in a single layer on a large baking pan; overcrowding will cause vegetables to steam rather than brown. Place in the oven and do not mess with it. Just roast until golden brown, 12 to 15 minutes. Remove and set aside.

RISOTTO

one 15-oz can whole
San Marzano
tomatoes

5 cups vegetable stock

1 tbsp unsalted butter

1 tbsp olive oil

2 small shallots, minced

6 cloves garlic, minced

1 cup Arborio rice

½ cup dry white wine

2 bay leaves

1 tbsp grated lemon zest

1 cup grated
Parmigiano-Reggiano
cheese, plus more
for serving

coarse salt and freshly
ground black pepper

- TO MAKE THE RISOTTO: Drain the liquid from the tomatoes into a saucepan and add the stock. Bring to a boil and lower the heat to a simmer. This mixture must be kept hot during the cooking process.

- Put the tomatoes in a bowl and mash them into chunks using the back of a wooden spoon. Don't pulverize, or the tomatoes will disintegrate into the risotto. Set aside.

- In a 6- or 8-quart stockpot, melt the butter with the olive oil over low heat. Add the shallots and garlic, cooking slowly until they almost look like a puree (called a sofrito). Do not brown. This will take about 10 minutes.

- Remove the sofrito, blot the pot with a paper towel, and return it to the stove over medium heat. Note the time on the clock. Add the rice and use a wooden spoon (the edges aren't sharp enough to damage the kernels) to move it around the pot so it toasts and starts to smell a little like nuts. It'll take 4 to 5 minutes. Add the wine and slowly cook it down, gently stirring. Add the sofrito, stirring to coat. Begin adding the hot stock mixture about ½ cup at a time, and stir after each addition until the liquid is absorbed so the rice loses its starch and thickens the mixture. Toss in the bay leaves after the third addition of stock; about 15 minutes into the cooking process, add the tomatoes. You might not end up using all the stock mixture.

- When the rice is cooked— 25 or 30 minutes total, although tasting is the best test—take the pot off the heat and gently stir in the ratatouille. Sprinkle in the zest to give it some brightness, and gently stir in the 1 cup cheese. Season with salt to taste. Transfer to serving plates and pass extra cheese and a pepper grinder on the side.

NOTE: Look for vegetables with a shiny exterior (which means they are freshly picked). The squash and eggplant should feel "tight" to the touch and not loaded with water or they'll get soggy.

TIP: Where a lot of people screw up is focusing on the al dente. Yes, the rice shouldn't be mush. But it also has to be cooked through. Here's my test. Let the rice drop off the spoon. It should not clump like oatmeal: It should fall in a smooth wave.

BUCATINI

Three Ways

Joey Campanaro | The Little Owl | New York City

MAKING FRESH PASTA IS a family activity—a few sets of hands mixing together a mountain of flour and eggs while a sauce slowly simmers on the stove. But there are times when I rely on a quality dried pasta (like De Cecco) and quick-cook pantry sauce, put together with mostly cupboard ingredients. For the sauces below, you may have to stop at the store and pick up a couple of peppers or a bunch of basil, but the inconvenience is minor compared with the flavor. Every ingredient counts: The riff on classic *amatriciana* turns smoky by swapping bacon for guanciale, the richness of browned butter needs the tangy punch of capers, and pickling the peppers cuts the oiliness of the anchovies. Be sure you cook the bucatini in abundantly salted water and plenty of it. As my dad says, "People should stick together, not pasta."

SERVES 4

DIFFICULTY:

EASY | REASONABLE | WORTH THE EFFORT

8 thick slices bacon, coarsely chopped

1 small white onion, sliced

1 garlic clove, smashed

½ **cup dry white wine**

one 28-oz can whole tomatoes, crushed with your hands, with juices

1 tsp red pepper flakes

1 tbsp chopped fresh flat-leaf parsley

4 torn fresh basil leaves

1 tbsp olive oil

1 lb bucatini pasta, cooked and drained

¼ cup grated pecorino romano cheese

BUCATINI WITH TOMATO AND BACON

- In a large skillet over medium-high heat, cook the bacon until slightly crisp, about 8 minutes.

- Pour off the excess fat, reserving about 2 tablespoons in the pan. Add the onion and garlic, stirring to coat with the fat. Cook until the onion is translucent, about 3 minutes. Add the white wine. It will immediately come to a boil. Cook to reduce by half, about 2 minutes. Add the tomatoes, crushed with your hands, including all the reserved liquid, plus the red pepper flakes. Lower the heat and simmer until thickened, about 20 minutes. Use a wooden spoon to break up the tomatoes, and stir the sauce occasionally to prevent sticking.

- Stir in the parsley, basil, and olive oil. When the basil becomes fragrant, add the drained pasta and take the pan off the heat. Sprinkle in the pecorino romano (Locatelli is my favorite), tossing well to coat.

BUCATINI WITH BROWN BUTTER, SPINACH, WALNUTS, AND CAPERS

DIFFICULTY:

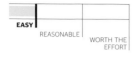

EASY | REASONABLE | WORTH THE EFFORT

1½ cups salted butter

juice of 1 lemon

1 tbsp drained capers

½ cup chopped walnuts

5 oz baby spinach

4 torn fresh sage leaves

1 lb bucatini pasta, cooked and drained

¼ cup grated Parmesan cheese

freshly ground black pepper

- In a small stockpot with high sides, melt the butter over medium heat. In order to brown the milk solids, all the water must be cooked out, so let the butter foam. Once it does, using a wooden spoon or wooden spatula, stir the butter (in a wave-like motion) to help the foam subside, and continue cooking until the butter is a beautiful amber color, 8 or 10 minutes. Stir occasionally to prevent the solids from sticking to the bottom of the pot. (The butter should look a little "sandy.")

- Once you get the butter where you want it, add the lemon juice to halt the browning. Lower the heat and add the capers and walnuts, letting their flavor infuse the butter for a minute. Turn off the heat and immediately add the spinach and sage leaves, tossing to wilt. Add the drained pasta and sprinkle in the Parmesan, tossing well to coat. Season with pepper.

BUCATINI WITH WHITE ANCHOVIES AND PEPPERS

DIFFICULTY:

EASY | REASONABLE | WORTH THE EFFORT

1 red bell pepper

1 green bell pepper

1 yellow bell pepper

1 tbsp sugar

¼ cup rice vinegar

1 to 2 tbsp olive oil

1 clove garlic, minced

12 white anchovies

3 torn fresh basil leaves

1 tbsp chopped fresh flat-leaf parsley

1 lb bucatini pasta, cooked and drained

¼ cup grated Parmesan cheese

¼ cup bread crumbs

freshly ground black pepper

- Halve, trim, and seed the peppers. Cut the peppers into thin strips. Whisk together the sugar and rice vinegar until the sugar dissolves. Toss the peppers with the vinegar and let the mixture sit for 1 hour, stirring occasionally to coat.

- In a large skillet over medium heat, heat the olive oil and lightly brown the clove. Add the white anchovies and stir to coat. Squeeze the excess vinegar from peppers and add them to the skillet, tossing to combine. Lower the heat and cook, stirring occasionally, until the peppers wilt and the flavors are infused, about 5 minutes. Take the pan off the heat and add the basil, parsley, and the drained pasta, tossing well to coat. Sprinkle in the Parmesan and bread crumbs and toss to combine. Season with pepper.

CONTINUED FROM

ESQUIRE
Classics

PRETTY EASY RECIPES FOR SOME OF THE BEST FISH DISHES OF ALL TIME.

Reprinted from the *Esquire Cookbook*, 1955

SHRIMP COOKED IN BEER

For 4, boil gently for about 15 minutes 4 cups of beer, 3 diced shallots, 2 medium onions minced fine, 3 ounces butter, a sprig of parsley, 1 bay leaf, 1 stalk of celery, and 6 peppercorns. Then add 2 pounds of peeled shrimp, turn the heat up, and cook for another 15 minutes. Season lightly with salt and $1/2$ teaspoon onion juice. Strain the sauce, lightly thicken with the beaten yolk of 1 egg, and pour it over the shrimp.

FILLET OF SOLE, ANYMAN

Put sole fillets, allowing 2 fillets or $1/2$ pound per person, in a pan with some butter, 1 tablespoon vinegar, a thin-sliced onion, salt, pepper, and 1 cup white wine. Cook for 10 minutes, covered. Meantime, sauté $1/2$ pound mushrooms in butter. After the fish has cooked, pour the mushrooms over it, add more wine, then bake in a moderate oven another 10 or 15 minutes.

DEVILED CRABS

For 4, dice 1 medium onion, $1/2$ green pepper, $1/2$ clove garlic, $1/2$ stalk celery, 1 tablespoon parsley. Sauté in $1/4$ pound butter until tender. Add 1 pound crumbled lump crab meat, $2/3$ cup cream, $1/4$ teaspoon thyme, 1 chopped hard-boiled egg, 2 raw eggs, $1 1/2$ tablespoons vinegar, $1/2$ teaspoon Worcestershire sauce, 10 drops Tabasco sauce, salt to taste. Heap into crab shells, top with 1 cup bread crumbs, dot with butter, and bake in a 375°F oven 10 to 15 minutes.

LOBSTER À LA NEWBURG

Boil one lobster, $1 1/2$ to 2 pounds, for each person. When cool, dice meat and add plenty of hot, clear butter, salt, and ground pepper. Fry without allowing it to take on color. Add 1 tablespoon lemon juice, cover with fresh cream, and reduce volume a little over low fire. Add 1 tablespoon Madeira for each lobster and bring to a lazy boil. Remove from fire. Thicken with 2 beaten egg yolks and same volume of cream, adding a little at a time and stirring briskly. Reheat without boiling, season with a pinch of cayenne, and salt to taste. Serve at once over wedges of toasted bread.

SHRIMP WITH RICE
FRA DIAVOLO

FOR THE RICE: Slice 2 small onions and cook them until golden in $1/4$ pound sweet butter. Add 1 quart capon (or chicken) broth and bring to a boil. Stir in 2 cups rice and cook for 20 minutes, to reduce the volume of broth.

FOR THE SHRIMP: Brown 3 diced garlic cloves in 4 tablespoons olive oil; then add a $1 1/2$-pound can of plum tomatoes, $1/2$ teaspoon pepper, $1/4$ teaspoon oregano, and 1 teaspoon chopped parsley. Cook for 15 minutes, then add $1 1/2$ pounds of peeled raw shrimp and simmer for 10 minutes.

Place rice on platter, cover with shrimp and sauce, and serve to 4, amply.

CHAPTER 4: SIDES

RED BLISS POTATO SALAD

Peter McAndrews | Modo Mio | Philadelphia

SERVES 4

DIFFICULTY:

EASY | REASONABLE | WORTH THE EFFORT

coarse salt

2½ lb Red Bliss potatoes, quartered

2 tbsp rinsed capers

½ cup thinly sliced roasted red peppers

2 cloves garlic, chopped

½ cup balsamic vinegar

2 tbsp sugar

1 tsp red pepper flakes

6 oil-packed anchovies, minced

1 cup extra-virgin olive oil

¼ cup chopped fresh mint, plus torn leaves for garnish

freshly ground black pepper

¼ cup grated Parmesan cheese

- Season a pot of water with enough salt so that it tastes like sea-water and bring it to a boil. Add the potatoes and cook until fork-tender, about 12 minutes. Drain and transfer to a mixing bowl.

- Stir in the following: capers, peppers, garlic, balsamic vinegar, sugar, red pepper flakes, and anchovies. (Use these even if you think you hate anchovies. They add a salty backbone, and any fishiness disappears into the dish.) Stir and let cool to room temperature.

- Add the olive oil and ¼ cup mint, then season with salt and pepper. Taste as you go—seasoning is personal. Sprinkle the Parmesan cheese and a few more torn mint leaves on top. Serve at room temperature. (It gets better after a day or two.)

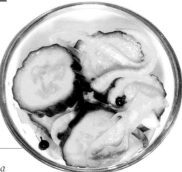

Bread 'n' Butter
PICKLES

Hugh Acheson | Five and Ten | Athens, Georgia

12 small (3-inch) Kirby cucumbers, or 2 English cucumbers

1 large sweet onion

½ cup coarse salt

leaves from 1 bunch celery

¼ tsp red pepper flakes

¼ tsp ground fenugreek

½ tsp ground turmeric

1 tsp brown mustard seeds

8 allspice berries

1½ cups cider vinegar

1 cup sugar

¼ cup maple syrup

• This is a simple recipe, and the result has tons more flavor than the store-boughts. Less sweet, more zesty. Wash the Kirby cucumbers under cold water and then slice into ⅓-inch rounds, about as thick as an Oreo. Peel the onion, cut in half lengthwise, and slice into semicircles the same width as the cukes. Toss the onions and the cucumbers in a bowl with the salt and let sit for 1 hour. Rinse well in a colander, drain, and place in a nonreactive bowl. Tear up the celery leaves and add to the mix, then set aside.

• In a saucepan, combine the pepper flakes, fenugreek, turmeric, mustard seeds, the allspice berries, vinegar, ½ cup water, the sugar, and maple syrup. Bring to a rapid boil and then pour over the cucumbers. Leave them uncovered for 2 hours and then refrigerate. When they reach fridge temperature, cover with plastic wrap. Done. But they'll be at their best a day or two later. They'll keep in the refrigerator for about 10 days.

SUBSTITUTE: You can use store-bought pickling spice instead of the allspice and preceding four ingredients, and you'll end up with good pickles, but not these pickles. And these pickles are better.

TWO STEAKHOUSE SIDES

Matt Hill | Charlie Palmer Steak | Washington, D.C.

MAKING SIDE DISHES for a steakhouse menu isn't about variety, it's about universal appeal. Steakhouse sides are typically served in larger portions because they're designed to stand alone, rather than enhance different proteins. Because there is a standard menu of classics, what sets each steakhouse's dishes apart is not only technique but ingredient quality and perfection of seasoning. My biggest challenge is resisting the urge to put bacon in every single side.

SERVES 6

DIFFICULTY:

EASY | REASONABLE | WORTH THE EFFORT

1½ lb Russian banana fingerling potatoes

2 tbsp olive oil

coarse salt and freshly ground black pepper

1 tbsp unsalted butter

3 oz pancetta, diced

2 shallots, sliced

2 tbsp fresh sage leaves, chiffonade

½ cup veal demi-glace

POTATOES WITH PANCETTA

- Preheat the oven to 400°F. Wash and dry the potatoes. Cut the potatoes in half lengthwise and toss with the olive oil, a pinch or two of salt, and a few grinds of black pepper. Place the seasoned potatoes, cut-side down, on a baking sheet and roast in the oven until golden brown and tender but not soft, about 20 minutes.

- While the potatoes are roasting, add the butter and pancetta to a large sauté pan over medium heat and render the pancetta until golden brown, 6 to 8 minutes. Add the shallots and lower the heat, cooking only until shallots are tender, about 2 minutes. Add the roasted potatoes and sage leaves (from the French, meaning "made of rags," chiffonade is a technique for cutting leafy vegetables and herbs; stack and tightly roll the sage leaves, and use a sharp knife to cut across—or kitchen shears to snip—the leaves into ribbons) and season with salt and pepper, going easy on the salt because the pancetta is aggressively seasoned. Add the demi-glace (robust flavor, syrupy consistency, available premade in many butcher departments), stirring to coat the potatoes, and cook until heated through and flavors marry, about 2 minutes.

SERVES 6

DIFFICULTY:

EASY | REASONABLE | WORTH THE EFFORT

2½ lb spinach, stemmed

1 tbsp extra-virgin olive oil

1 clove garlic, chopped

2 shallots, minced

2 tbsp unsalted butter

3 tbsp all-purpose flour

2 cups heavy cream

¼ tsp freshly grated nutmeg

⅓ cup grated Parmesan cheese

coarse salt and freshly ground black pepper

CREAMED SPINACH

- Thoroughly wash the spinach in cold water and drain in a colander. (The spinach should still be damp but not wet.) It takes a mountain of raw spinach to cook down into 6 portions, so you'll need a large heavy-bottomed pot, like an 8-quart stockpot. Add the olive oil to the pan and cook the garlic and shallots over low heat until translucent, about 1 minute. Add the spinach a few handfuls at a time, stirring to wilt down the leaves after each addition. When all the spinach is wilted, transfer to a colander and drain, shaking the colander gently to remove excess liquid.

- Using the same pot, melt the butter. Sprinkle in the flour, whisking constantly until a paste forms. This is when a flat sauce whisk (rather than a round whisk) comes in handy because the shape and its flexible wires allow you to scrape together the butter and flour—the reason it's also called a roux whisk. Cook the paste until it begins to smell a little like toasted nuts, a minute or so. Slowly add the cream, whisking to incorporate and prevent lumps. Add the nutmeg (the best flavor comes from grating a whole nutmeg on the extra-fine side of a box grater rather than using ground nutmeg from a jar) and cook until the cream begins to thicken and the flour taste is gone, about 3 minutes. Add half of the Parmesan, stirring to combine.

- Return the spinach to the pot. Season with salt and pepper and serve, sprinkled with the remaining cheese.

Duck-Fat

POTATOES

From the Esquire *kitchen*

SERVES 4

DIFFICULTY:

EASY | REASONABLE | WORTH THE EFFORT

¼ **cup duck fat (see Note)**

1 lb small red new potatoes (about 16), with a strip peeled around center

coarse salt and freshly ground black pepper

- Over low heat, melt the duck fat in a deep skillet with a tight-fitting lid. Raise the temperature to heat. Run the potatoes under water, letting the excess drain through a colander. Transfer to the skillet (water and hot fat create splatter but also cooking steam; the potatoes must be in one layer with enough room to roll around) and quickly cover. Shake the pan slightly to coat the potatoes and cook until deep golden and tender, about 18 minutes. Season abundantly with salt and pepper and serve.

NOTE: Rendered duck fat is available at specialty markets or from D'Artagnan (dartagnan.com). It costs around $5 for 7 ounces.

Twice-Baked
POTATOES

Charlie Palmer | Charlie Palmer Steak | Las Vegas

SERVES 2

DIFFICULTY:

EASY		
	REASONABLE	WORTH THE EFFORT

kosher or coarse salt

2 Idaho potatoes

olive oil

3 oz fresh goat cheese, at room temperature

2 tbsp sour cream

freshly ground black pepper

½ cup scallion greens thinly sliced on diagonal

• Preheat the oven to 350°F. Make two beds of salt in a shallow pan. Rub the potatoes lightly with oil and place each on a salt mound. (Now you won't need to turn the potatoes to avoid scorch marks from hot pan. Crinkled-up aluminum foil also works.) Bake until fork-tender, about 55 minutes; remove and let the potatoes cool until you can handle them.

• Peel one potato, coarsely chop, and place in a bowl. Cut the other potato in half lengthwise. Leaving shells about ¼ inch thick, scoop out insides of both halves and add the insides to a bowl. Mash the warm potatoes with a fork, mixing in the cheese and sour cream, and season with salt and pepper. Fold in the scallions and scoop into the shells. (Leaving the surface a little uneven forms nice browned peaks under the broiler.) Broil 6 to 8 inches from the heat until the potatoes are heated through and golden, about 4 minutes.

Keens

HASH BROWNS

Bill Rodgers | Keens Steakhouse | New York City

SERVES 2

DIFFICULTY:

EASY | **REASONABLE** | WORTH THE EFFORT

¾ lb small Yukon gold potatoes (about 4), washed but not peeled

1½ tbsp coarse salt

1 tbsp canola oil

1 tbsp unsalted butter

½ cup diced Spanish onion, or other mild onion

1 tbsp chopped garlic (about 2 cloves)

1 tsp chopped fresh thyme

1 tsp chopped fresh rosemary

2 tsp chopped fresh flat-leaf parsley

freshly ground black pepper

- Preheat the oven to 400°F. Put the potatoes in a pot, cover with cold water by 2 inches, add 1 tablespoon salt, and bring to a simmer.

- While the potatoes are cooking (they'll take about 30 minutes), heat half the oil and butter in a small sauté pan over medium heat. Add the onion, garlic, and remaining ½ tablespoon salt and cook until the onion begins to caramelize, about 8 minutes. Set aside.

- When the potatoes are cooked (a toothpick inserted should offer no resistance), drain them and put in a large bowl. Add the onion mixture and herbs and mix with a wooden spoon just until the potatoes break up and the onions and herbs are incorporated. (It should be chunky.) Add pepper to taste. With your hands, form 2 loose patties (or more, if there's enough mixture) about the size of your palm.

- In a nonstick pan, heat the remaining ½ tablespoon each oil and butter until foamy. Add the hash browns and brown on one side, 3 to 4 minutes. Flip to the other side and place in oven until the second side is crisp, 8 to 10 minutes.

THE ESQUIRE GUIDE TO
OFF-SEASON
GRILLING

WHO MADE THE RULE THAT YOUR GRILL MUST BE IN LOCKDOWN FROM LABOR DAY TO MEMORIAL DAY? HERE ARE A FEW IDEAS THAT WILL KEEP THE FIRE GOING THROUGH THE COLDEST MONTHS. STEP ONE: SHOVEL A PATH OUT THE BACK DOOR.

GRILLED APPLES

Peel, core, and halve a few Fuji apples, brush the flat sides lightly with canola oil, and season with a pinch of salt and pepper. Place on the grill directly over heat and cook each side for about 3 minutes. Then move them to the side, away from the direct heat, close the lid, and cook for another 5 minutes.

GRILLED BACON

Place ½-inch-thick slices of slab bacon directly on grill, adjusting the grate so the bacon is as far from the direct heat as possible. Watch carefully—it won't take long to cook, a few minutes per side, maybe. Pull the bacon off the grill, brush with maple syrup, and top with cracked black pepper.

GRILLED GROG

In a small saucepan, combine 4 ounces dark rum, 2 ounces brandy, 8 lumps sugar, 4 slices lemon, and 2 cups coffee. Place on the grill and heat until simmering. Ladle into 4 mugs, one of which is for you to drink while tending the meat.

BAKED CRANBERRY BEANS

with Parmesan

Billy Grant | Grants | West Hartford, Connecticut

SERVES 6

DIFFICULTY:

EASY | **REASONABLE** | WORTH THE EFFORT

1 lb dried cranberry beans, or navy or pinto beans

4 oz pancetta, or 4 slices slab bacon, diced

2 medium yellow onions, diced

1/2 cup extra-virgin olive oil, plus more for drizzling

1/2 bulb fennel, diced

coarse salt and freshly ground black pepper

1 cup canned diced plum tomatoes

6 cloves roasted garlic (see Note)

1 sprig fresh thyme

1 sprig fresh rosemary

1 tbsp chopped fresh flat-leaf parsley

1 bay leaf

4 cups chicken broth

1 bunch escarole, washed and coarsely chopped

1/2 cup grated Parmesan cheese

1/4 cup panko (Japanese bread crumbs)

- Baked beans were a treat on special-occasion Sundays, when my family took a break from spaghetti and meatballs. It's easy: The night before, put the beans into a bowl and cover with water. Soak for 8 to 10 hours.

- Cook the pancetta in a 6-quart stockpot over medium heat until crisp. Add the onions, 1/2 cup olive oil, and the fennel. Cook slowly for about 20 minutes. Season with salt and pepper.

- Add the tomatoes, roasted garlic, drained beans, thyme, rosemary, parsley, and bay leaf. Stir to coat, add the broth, and simmer for 1 1/2 hours, or until the beans are tender.

- Preheat the oven to 350°F. Add the escarole. Sprinkle with half of the Parmesan cheese. Transfer to a 4-quart baking dish, top with the remaining Parmesan, a drizzle of olive oil, and the panko, and bake for 60 to 90 minutes, until bubbling.

NOTE: To learn how to roast garlic, see page 53. Roasted garlic is also available in jars, but don't buy any that's been flavored.

ASPARAGUS

From the Esquire *kitchen*

SERVES 1 OR MORE

DIFFICULTY:

EASY | REASONABLE | WORTH THE EFFORT

asparagus (as much as you want to cook)

olive oil for drizzling

sea salt and cracked black pepper

Pecorino Romano cheese (optional)

- Snap off the bottom of each asparagus spear: About an inch from the base, break it like you're snapping a twig, and the bottom will come off easily. Rinse the asparagus and soak in a bowl of water for a few minutes to remove any dirt, then pat dry.

- Lay the asparagus on a baking sheet and drizzle with olive oil, coating all the spears. (They shouldn't be sitting in a puddle of oil, use just barely enough to make them look slick.) Sprinkle with salt and pepper. At this point, the asparagus is ready to cook.

- Cooking options:

  · Roast in a preheated 400°F oven for about 12 minutes, or

  · Cook over high heat in a large pan for about 10 minutes, or

  · Grill on a hot grill for about 8 minutes.

- Serve with shaved or grated cheese, if you want.

TIP: The goal is to cook them until they're just short of floppy. Cooking times will vary depending on the width of the asparagus.

BROILED BROCCOLI

Barton Seaver | *Chef and cookbook author*

WE'VE BECOME SLAVES TO words like *local*, *fresh*, and *seasonal*. We all want to be Thomas Jefferson's agrarian hero, but sustainable food is a difficult beast. You want to save the oceans? Eat more broccoli. Change the topography of your plate. Sixteen ounces of shrimp on a plate is not the best nutrition. And you don't have to eat farmers'-market organic broccoli or participate in some green revolution. Just eat broccoli. They have it at Walmart. Eat some shrimp, but let's make broccoli and beans more delicious. Restaurants stress the protein. People read menu items left to right, with the protein first. I read descriptions right to left. Broiled vegetables are the future.

SERVES 1 OR MORE

DIFFICULTY:

broccoli, cut into florets

mayonnaise

coarse salt and freshly ground black pepper

chili powder or ground cumin (optional)

- Simmer broccoli in salted water until it's tender. Take it out, put it on a baking sheet, put a drop of mayonnaise on top of each piece, and put it under the broiler for a couple of minutes until it's crisp, even a little burned. Season with salt and pepper. Throw some chili powder on it if you want. Or cumin. It's awesomely delicious. I can't make it any easier for you.

MACARONI PIE

Amanda Cohen | Dirt Candy | New York City

WHEN MOST PEOPLE say "mac and cheese," they think of creamy cheese sauce and macaroni noodles. But for me, mac and cheese will always be macaroni pie, a dish I learned about when I visited my husband's family in South Carolina. It's the one thing he makes on a regular basis—a big slab of it appears in the fridge once a month and we carve off slices and eat it cold, slathered in hot sauce. If we're feeling particularly sophisticated, we reheat it. Basically, it's a macaroni and cheese casserole, and the beauty is that all the measurements are by eye, so it doesn't scare noncooks.

SERVES 6

DIFFICULTY:

EASY	REASONABLE	WORTH THE EFFORT

one 1-lb box macaroni noodles

8 oz Cheddar cheese

milk, to cover noodles

- Preheat the oven to 350°F. Cook the noodles according to the instructions on the box.

- Grease any baking dish or pie pan you have on hand, and pour in the noodles once they're done. Cube the block of Cheddar (or two blocks, or twelve) and mix with the noodles, making sure that a lot of the cheese winds up on top. Then pour in enough milk (skim, whole, 2%—it actually doesn't matter) until you can see the milk rising up through the noodles.

- Throw it in the oven and let it bake until the top starts to brown. And that's it.

SUBSTITUTE: To make it fancy, add smoked Cheddar and grate more cheese over the top to get a thick bubbling, crispy, golden brown crust. Cook it longer to make the top crispier, cook it shorter to keep it soupy, add sausage to the mix if that's your thing, throw in a tomato if you want to pretend it's healthy. Use mozzarella, smoked Gouda, Monterey Jack—whatever cheese is your current romantic partner. The result is a moist pie with lots of pockets of oozing cheese studded throughout, and a crispy crust of crunchy macaroni and melted cheese.

GARLIC BREAD

two ways

From the Esquire *kitchen*

SERVES 4

DIFFICULTY:

EASY | REASONABLE | WORTH THE EFFORT

4 oz unsalted butter, very soft

3 cloves garlic, smashed and chopped

1 tbsp finely chopped parsley or chives

1 loaf Italian bread

⅓ cup freshly grated Parmesan cheese (for crispy version only)

- SOFT: Preheat the oven to 350°F. Using a spoon, mix the butter, garlic, and parsley in a small bowl. Slice the bread crossways into individual pieces, and spread some of the butter mixture between every other slice. Wrap the bread loosely in foil, sealing the top like a tent, and place it in oven for 15 minutes.

- CRISPY: Preheat the oven to 350°F. Slice the bread horizontally into two large halves and place them, cut-side up, on a sturdy baking sheet. Using a spoon, mix the butter, garlic, and parsley in a small bowl. Spread the butter mixture evenly on both halves and place them in the oven for 10 to 12 minutes. Remove the bread from the oven and sprinkle it with Parmesan cheese. Set the oven to broil and place the oven rack in the upper third of the oven. Broil the bread for a minute or two, until the cheese and the edges start to toast, then remove immediately. (It burns easily.)

Truffled

MACARONI AND CHEESE

Michael Mina | Stripsteak | Las Vegas

SERVES 2

DIFFICULTY:

EASY		
	REASONABLE	WORTH THE EFFORT

1 lb elbow macaroni

2 tbsp canola oil

2 bone-in skinless chicken thighs

coarse salt and freshly ground black pepper

3 tbsp all-purpose flour, plus more for dredging

1 yellow onion, sliced

1 clove garlic, smashed

small bunch fresh thyme

4 cups chicken stock

2 cups heavy cream

¾ cup grated Asiago cheese

3 rounded tbsp grated Parmesan cheese

1 rounded tbsp crumbled blue cheese

1 tbsp white-truffle oil, or more to taste

- Cook the macaroni according to the instructions on the package. Set aside.

- In a heavy-bottomed pot, heat the canola oil over medium heat. Season the chicken with salt and pepper, dredge in flour, and add to the pot. Brown the chicken, turning once, 3 to 4 minutes. Remove and set aside (not fully cooked at this point).

- Add the onion, garlic, and thyme and cook until the onion is translucent, 4 to 5 minutes. Add the 3 tablespoons flour and cook, stirring frequently, for another 2 minutes. Return the chicken to the pot, add stock, and bring to a simmer, scraping the bottom of the pot to remove any brown bits. Simmer gently to thicken, about 15 minutes. Remove the thighs, now fully cooked, and set aside.

- Whisk the cream into the sauce and simmer to thicken, at least 5 minutes. Strain the sauce into a large bowl (discarding the onion, garlic, and thyme sprigs) and whisk in the cheeses immediately. Pick the chicken meat from the bones and stir into the sauce, along with the macaroni. Season to taste. Just before serving, stir in the truffle oil.

See photo on page 95.

MY MOM COULDN'T COOK

By Tom Junod

MY MOTHER, FRANCES JUNOD, was not just a mother, not just a mom. She was a dame. She was a broad. She went through her entire life as a Harlow-esque platinum blonde, and I never knew the real color of her hair. She liked to go to the track, and she liked to go out to restaurants. She did not like to cook. That she did it anyway—that she had no choice—owed itself to generational expectations, and to the fact that if my mother was a doll, in the Runyon-esque sense of the word, my father was a guy, a pinky-ringed sharpie who spent many nights going to the New York City restaurants my mother longed to frequent, but who, on nights when he came home, loudly expected food on the table. So my mother put food on the table. She cooked three hundred nights a year.

She cooked spaghetti with butter and cheese. She cooked hamburgers, panfried without added fat on a hot, salted cast-iron skillet, until they formed a hard crust. She cooked scrambled eggs, made idiosyncratic by the addition of a teaspoon of water. She cooked shell steaks sprinkled with salt and Ac'cent—MSG—and she cooked chicken parts lathered in a sweet-sour sauce called Saucy Susan. For dessert she made Junket or Jell-O or My-T-Fine chocolate pudding.

I had to like her cooking, and I did, as long as she observed the Mashed Potato Rule. The Mashed Potato Rule, simply stated, is this: There is no such thing as bad mashed potatoes as long as they're actually potatoes, mashed. We had mashed potatoes a lot—I can still see the blood from my hamburger running into them on my plate—and it didn't matter that they were lumpy and grainy and that my mother had no talent for making them; they were *Edenic* so long as she did. I loved them, as I loved her. But while on my plate they formed the barrier between the battleship-gray lamb chops and the olive-drab green beans, in my heart they formed the barrier between the discovery that my mother hated cooking and the altogether different discovery that my mother hated

cooking so much that she even hated cooking for me.

See, I had figured that my mother hated cooking for the obvious reason that she hated cooking for my father. She could never satisfy him. Indeed, she hated cooking for him so much that he kept their marriage intact by absolving her of the responsibility—by taking her with him to Roosevelt Raceway, where they ate at the Cloud Casino while I stayed home and panfried a shell steak. I was in high school, stoned and rapacious and suddenly free to be disloyal, by which I mean I was suddenly free to tell the truth. Like most human beings, I grew up making the connection between food and love; what I began to realize when I started cooking for myself was that the more necessary connection was between food and honesty. "Oh, I'm a terrible fibber," my mother would say and then blithely assert that she'd spent "hours over a hot stove" cooking the package of frozen Banquet fried-chicken drumsticks on our plates. She'd say this with a knowing cackle that served simultaneously as an admission of guilt and a warning that we must never say that she was guilty. Food was love all right, and we had to tell my mom that we loved her by swallowing a fiction that everybody knew was untrue.

I was still in high school when my mother first broke the Mashed Potato Rule. From another perspective: I was in high school when I first broke the rule that if food was to be love, then so was the obligation to accept my mother's untruths about it. Me: Ma (I always called her Ma), what's with the potatoes? My mother: What's wrong with the potatoes? Me: They're not potatoes. They came from a box. My mother: So what if they come from a box? They're still potatoes. Me: They're not potatoes! My mother: *You can't tell the difference.*

And with that my mother uttered the signal words of my culinary existence. I could tell the difference, and I spent the rest of my life proving that I could. Just as my mother had come to the conclusion that *It's not worth it,*

I was coming to the conclusion that *It is*.

My mother was a good mother. I was a good son. My mother was a betrayed woman—I think I knew that from an early age—and so I was careful never to betray her, as she, by instinct, never betrayed me. But now I felt betrayed, and I betrayed her in return by learning to cook. I am my family's cook now. I cook three hundred days a year and have cooked three hundred days a year for years. When my mother would visit, I would make her chop, according to specification. "How's this?" she'd ask, showing me the cutting board of haphazardly chopped broccoli, and when I'd say she had to chop it smaller, finer, more uniformly, she'd say, "You're some pain in the ass," or "What a pill." I was perversely proud of her exasperation. My mother wasn't college-educated, but she wasn't stupid, either. She knew what was going on.

And yet hunger won out, as it always does in human affairs. On Sunday nights, after my parents also moved to Atlanta, we'd have them over for Sunday supper—itself a term that seemed the province of a family not my own—and I'd serve pot roast, the one meal that, as any novice cook knows, obeys its own variant of the Mashed Potato Rule: There's no such thing as a bad pot roast as long as you put enough stuff in the pot and you roast it long enough. But my mother didn't know. She'd come to our house, and because she'd become too old and uncertain to chop, she'd watch me do the work and laugh to herself, as was her habit. "What are you laughing at, Ma?" "Nothing. Just laughin'." But she was interested not just in what she still regarded as my folly but in what made my folly *worth* it—what made the food good. "What kind of meat do you use?" she always asked, and when I wondered why she wanted to know, she said, "Well, it's always so tender." And that's when I knew what I wasn't supposed to know all along: My mother didn't know how to cook. She didn't know the rule that can get you through just about any meal: If it's tender, cook it fast over high heat; if it's tough, cook it slow over low.

> "Oh, I'm a terrible fibber," my mother would say and then blithely assert that she'd spent "hours over a hot stove" cooking the package of frozen Banquet fried-chicken drumsticks on our plates.

I thought, for a long time, that my mother hated cooking because she was a bad cook, because she rejected cooking as a way of rejecting us, because she was, at heart, a liar. Now I understood that she hated cooking because she didn't know how to do it and so had no idea how a meal might turn out.

Did she forgive me? Did she forgive me for being a pill and a pain in the ass—for taking my father's side? I know damned well she never thought of it that way. I was her son, after all, and I was a good egg. But that's how I thought of it, and I can tell you that the narrative arc of a life is more unforgiving than a mother could ever be. After my father died, my mother went into assisted living—or to be more precise and unsparing, I put her there. And she flourished, though food was always an issue. "Ma, eat something." "I'm not hungry." "C'mon. The food's not bad"—and to prove it, I'd eat platefuls of it. "It stinks," she'd say, and that was that. One day, in her ninety-second year, she simply stopped eating, and when she went to the hospital for intravenous fluids, she suffered a stroke that deprived her of her ability to feed herself. I had a conversation with her gerontologist, in which he told me the way she would die, in which he told me that unless she was fed via feeding tube she would die of the complications of malnutrition—of hunger. He didn't want to give her a feeding tube. Neither did I, versed as I was in the letter and spirit of her living will and her medical directives. But I never asked her about it. I never told her that we planned for her to die. I simply went every day, and tried to spoon-feed her cottage cheese that dribbled from her mouth like sand. I even cooked for her—the spaghetti with butter and cheese that was the first food I ever loved; the pot roast that was the last food she ever called delicious. I was the family cook, which meant that I was driven to preserve my family by making them care about something they had to do: eat. But my mother didn't have to care anymore. She didn't even have to eat. The family cook, I fed her tenderly to the last, and she starved to death.

CHAPTER 5

Dessert

The only dessert you'll ever need:

FRUIT CRISP

Reprinted from *Esquire Eats*, 2004

BY FRANCINE MAROUKIAN

IF ANYONE ASKS, a cobbler is a baked fruit dish with a top crust made from sweetened biscuit dough. A fruit crisp, on the other hand, has a crumbly, streusel-like topping (usually made from flour, sugar, and butter; this version also has nuts). Now, which do you think is easier? There is no reason—absolutely none—that exempts you from being able to make a crisp. If you don't have a food processor, the ingredients for the topping can be placed in a large bowl and rubbed between your fingers until the warmth of your skin softens the butter and a lumpy paste begins to form. Fruit crisps are a mainstay American dessert, and although dunce-cap easy, they deliver a simple but stunning dessert statement: "Yes, I made it myself."

If there's any secret, it is to pick fresh, ripe (but still slightly firm) fruit that provides true flavor. If the fruit didn't taste good going into the oven, it won't taste good coming out.

SERVES 4

DIFFICULTY:

EASY	REASONABLE	WORTH THE EFFORT

STACKING TEXTURES/ SERVING OPTIONS

FOR COLD-WEATHER CRISPS, like pear and apple, serve warm from the oven with whipped cream or ice cream, changing the flavorings to suit the fruit.

Serve cold apple or pear crisps with warm butterscotch sauce and whipped cream.

FOR SUMMER CRISPS, like plum or peach, serve cold, with whipped cream or ice cream, changing the flavorings to flatter the filling.

Serve plum or peach crisp warm from the oven for a summer weekend breakfast.

FOR THE TOPPING

½ cup unbleached
all-purpose flour

½ cup firmly packed
light brown sugar

½ cup shelled walnuts

5 tbsp unsalted butter,
chilled

FOR THE FILLING

½ cup dried fruit
(see **Tip**)

1 tbsp liquor, nut or
fruit liqueur, or brandy
(see **Tip**)

4½ cups fresh
fruit (pears, peaches,
apples, or plums),
unpeeled, in small
(about ½-inch) dice

2 tbsp lemon juice

1 tsp vanilla extract

1 tbsp unbleached
all-purpose flour

1 tbsp granulated
sugar

pinch of ground
nutmeg

pinch of ground
cinnamon

pinch of ground
allspice

- Place the flour, sugar, and walnuts in a food processor and process until combined (use quick pulses, the nuts should not be ground). Cut the butter into small pieces and add to the food process, pulsing until a lumpy paste is formed (about 30 seconds). Refrigerate until ready to use.

- Place the dried fruit in a small heatproof bowl and cover with boiling water. Set aside until the fruit softens and plumps, about 30 minutes. Drain the water and toss the fruit with the liquor, liqueur, or brandy.

- Place the fresh fruit in a large mixing bowl, sprinkle with lemon juice, and toss. Add the vanilla and toss again. Sprinkle in the dried fruit with its liquid and toss to evenly distribute. Sprinkle the flour, sugar, and spices over the fruit and toss to coat. Let the fruit mixture stand at room temperature (to draw out natural juices) for at least 30 minutes.

- Preheat the oven to 400°F. Place the rack in the upper third of the oven.

- Spoon the fruit into a 9 x 9-inch ovenproof glass baking dish. Crumble the cold topping over the fruit and bake until the topping is crisp and browned and the fruit is bubbling around the edges, about 30 minutes. If serving cold, cool to room temperature, then cover with plastic wrap and refrigerate.

NOTE: The flavor and sweetness of fruit vary from tart to bland to stupendous, depending on the season and variety. Taste the apples, pears, peaches, or plums before you start, and adjust the amounts of dried fruit, sugar, spices, and other seasonings to boost the overall flavor, sweetness, or tartness as needed. (Be warned, though, there is no such thing as "adding less.") To serve 8, double the recipe and use a 13 x 9-inch ovenproof glass baking dish.

TIP: Be inventive: Use golden raisins and sun-dried cherries or cranberries for the apple crisp; apricots and figs (cut into small pieces) for the pear; sun-dried blueberries for the plum crisp; and sun-dried strawberries mixed with golden raisins for the peach. Match the flavoring to the fruit: Try Calvados for apple crisp, cassis for plum, dark rum for pear, and bourbon or Frangelico for peach.

CHAPTER 6: DRINKS *(with Food)*

THINGS A MAN SHOULD KNOW ABOUT
WINE AND SPIRITS

By David Wondrich

Try some prosecco or Champagne at the beginning of the night. It's light and acidic, and acidity starts saliva dripping. That gets you thinking of food. It's also festive. It dances around on your palate a little. You're celebrating the end of the working day and the beginning of relaxation time.

Unless it's a business dinner, in which case you're just trying to get a couple quick ones under your belt so you can sit through the damn thing. In that case I recommend martinis.

Sherry is also a good, underrated way to start a meal. A glass of chilled fino ("fine") or Manzanilla sherry is rocking. It's drier than anything ever made because it ages under a crust of yeast, which eats up all the natural sugar in the wine. That stuff is bone dry. As an aperitif, it's amazing.

Wine is a drink you have with food. I don't really consider it recreational.

If there's a good wine store in your neighborhood, shop there until you know the people—and whether to trust their recommendations.

For the meal: Red wine with meat, white with fish—it's a rule of thumb, but like all rules of thumb, it's made to be broken.

Just know what you're doing. Fish tends to be subtle in flavor, and red wines can be big and overpowering, so you don't necessarily want to kill your food with wine. And you don't want your steak to clobber a really nice delicate white wine.

But again, it's not a law. Whatever you're in the mood for.

There's no law that says you have to serve red wine warm.

If it's a big, cheap, red table wine, I've been known to put an ice cube in it if it's too warm. Relax. It's okay.

You can also throw it in the freezer for ten minutes. Don't be afraid. It's wine. It's not like the communion wafer, although some people treat it like that.

Don't worry about the proper type of wineglass. In Europe you see those little water-glass-type things. I like those. They're sturdy and peasantlike.

A bottle of wine for every two people is sufficient, generally. If you're not doing cocktails and after-dinner drinks, then two bottles for every three people. And hope it stops there.

That's the problem with wine at dinner: If you've got a lot, people drink it unthinkingly. At least I do.

One drink after 10 P.M. equals two before 10 P.M. One drink after 4 A.M. equals—well, it scarcely matters. If you're up drinking at 4 A.M., you're screwed anyway.

A very expensive wine and a very good wine are not necessarily synonymous.

After dinner, there is nothing like a glass of really rich, old port that you can sit and chew over. It's the Scotch whisky of wines. And the dessert-wine landscape is a wonderful place to experiment.

On to the hard stuff: Using very expensive liquors for mixing cocktails is generally not a good idea. You're not getting your money's worth. There are a few small exceptions—personal preferences you may deem worth it. But finding those is costly.

Making somebody a drink is a friendly gesture in any country in the world.

When stirring a cocktail, crack the ice and use as much as you can get in the glass. You end up with this super-cooled slurry that's actually less watered-down than if you had spent a long time trying to get it cold with cubes of ice. It's counterintuitive. But the chipped ice has more surface area.

You can use anything to crack ice. It will make a little mess, but it's only ice. You can, if you're doing a lot, get a canvas bag and a carpenter's mallet—which is much more fun than anything else involving mixing drinks short of setting them on fire.

If you're drinking something that's really lovely and you just want to keep it cold while you drink it, use the biggest block of ice you can fit in the glass.

A good trick: In an Old-Fashioned or a Manhattan, crack a few cubes and put a couple of whole cubes in—this dilutes the drink a little, but not too much, and keeps it cold for a while.

American whiskeys and bourbons are distilled with ice in mind—they're big-flavored and usually bottled at a reasonably high proof. They laugh at ice. They want ice.

But a good single-malt Scotch—unless it's cask-strength, try it neat. Maybe a drop of cool water. Perfect.

People fetishize cocktail making, but mixing drinks is really systems engineering. Think through all the steps beforehand and you'll rarely get into trouble.

Ever try making an Old-Fashioned using tequila instead of rye or bourbon? Do. It's a preparation that works great with almost any liquor. (See the recipe, page 200.)

There's no better Daiquiri recipe in the world than the juice of half a lime, a bar-spoonful of superfine sugar, stirred in, and 2 ounces of good white rum.

All things being equal, for mixing drinks you want a higher-proof spirit because it will come through the mix better. It'll be more pungent and rich and tasty.

A note on muddling: You can muddle with anything. A spoon is difficult, because it doesn't have much wide area. But I've used lipstick cases. I once used a souvenir 50-caliber machine gun casing. A screwdriver handle—just watch out for the other end, especially after the second round. Use the heel of your wife's shoe. It's like anything else. A man should be flexible.

If you don't have a shaker, hold two glasses together very tightly, with maybe a towel around the middle to catch the leaks. It's not ideal, but it works.

After dinner: Get a small glass and just barely cover the bottom with a good Scotch. A quarter-inch at a time. You can give yourself a status check with each refill. Eight very small glasses is better than one three-finger pour.

The digestive powers of certain after-dinner drinks may be a convenient fiction we all agree on so we can get some more booze under our belts. Not that there's anything wrong with that.

One guy who came over for dinner, I gave him a little glass of twenty-five-year-old Macallan, and he shot it. I thought—cough, cough—really? For the next drink, I slightly redefined "quality Scotch." Whatever. He enjoyed it. That's all that matters.

David Wondrich is *Esquire*'s drinks correspondent and the author of *Imbibe!*, *Killer Cocktails*, and *Esquire Drinks*.

FIVE ESSENTIAL COCKTAILS

By David Wondrich

MARTINI

THIS TECHNIQUE USED TO BE KNOWN as the "in and out" martini, or—if you were one of Ed McMahon's fellow USMC fighter pilots in Korea, the "McTini." (Yes, *that* Ed McMahon.) However you make it, if you garnish your martini with a cocktail onion, it becomes a Gibson (although this was originally made with Plymouth gin; try it, the stuff is still around). If you should happen to have some excess absinthe on hand, a couple of drops will transform that Gibson into a Third Degree (the driest of the traditional martini variants, with a ratio of 7:1). And if you do find that Plymouth gin, mix it 2-to-1 with French vermouth, tip in a couple dashes of orange bitters, and you've got a Hoffman House—with a twist, please. (New York's Hoffman House, on Twenty-fourth Street across from Madison Square, was famous for the stupendous nakedness of its bar nude and the superlative quality of its drinks; in fact, this is our favorite martini variant, although if we can't find Plymouth we'll use Tanqueray and make it 1:1.)

SERVES 1

1 oz dry vermouth

4 oz gin

1 olive for garnish

GLASS TYPE: COCKTAIL GLASS

- Fill a metal shaker with cracked ice. Pour in the dry vermouth (we prefer Noilly Prat), stir briefly, and strain out (this may be discarded). Add the gin (we prefer Beefeater, Tanqueray, Junípero—you want it around 94 proof). Stir briskly for about 10 seconds, strain into a chilled cocktail glass, and garnish with the olive.

MANHATTAN

OF COURSE, HUMAN BEINGS, being human beings, can never leave well enough alone. Here, then, are the obligatory variants. First, a few you can make by monkeying around with the bitters: Lose the angostura and pitch in a splash of Amer Picon and it's a Monahan; a splash of anisette and it's a Narragansett; 2 dashes of cherry brandy and a dash of absinthe and you've got a McKinley's Delight. Leave a dash of the angostura in, add a dash of orange bitters and 3 dashes of absinthe: a Sherman. Or you can tinker with the vermouth. Replace half the Italian vermouth with French for a so-called Perfect Manhattan. Equal parts rye, French vermouth, and Italian vermouth: a Jumbo. Make that with bourbon: a Honolulu (no bitters at all in those last two). Cut the Italian vermouth entirely and make it half bourbon and half French vermouth: a Rosemary. To turn that into a Brown University, just add a couple dashes of orange bitters. Coming almost full circle, if you make your classic 2-to-1 Manhattan with French vermouth instead of Italian and a dash of Amer Picon and one of maraschino, you're in Brooklyn. And there are more—the Rob Roy, for one, but we gotta stop somewhere.

SERVES 1

2 oz rye whiskey (see Tip)

1 oz Italian vermouth

2 dashes angostura bitters

1 lemon twist or maraschino cherry for garnish

GLASS TYPE: COCKTAIL GLASS

- Stir the rye, vermouth, and bitters well with cracked ice. A stirred drink will be silky smooth in texture and actually colder than a shaken one, provided you do take the trouble to crack the ice. Strain into a chilled cocktail glass and garnish with a twist of lemon peel or, of course, a maraschino cherry (which is subject to the same challenge re: purity as adding an olive to a martini).

  TIP: In case of emergency—you need a Manhattan and you're passing a bar of the "Rye? Nah." variety—opt for a high-proof bourbon over any other substitute. (Canadian "rye" is usually that in name only.)

CONTINUED →

GIMLET

SERVES 1

2 oz **London dry gin**

2/3 oz **Rose's lime juice**

GLASS TYPE: COCKTAIL GLASS

- Shake the gin and Rose's lime juice well with cracked ice, then strain into a chilled cocktail glass and serve.

SIDECAR

SERVES 1

3/4 oz **Cointreau**

1/2 to 3/4 oz **freshly squeezed lemon juice**

1 1/2 oz **cognac**

GLASS TYPE: COCKTAIL GLASS

- Shake the Cointreau, lemon juice, and cognac well with cracked ice, then strain into a chilled cocktail glass that has had its outside rim rubbed with lemon juice and dipped in sugar; serve.

OLD-FASHIONED

SERVES 1

1 **sugar cube**

2 or 3 dashes **angostura bitters**

water or club soda

1 **ice cube**

2 oz **rye whiskey or bourbon**

GLASS TYPE: OLD-FASHIONED GLASS

- Place the sugar cube (or 1/2 teaspoon loose sugar) in an Old-Fashioned, or rocks, glass. Wet it down with the angostura bitters and a short splash of water or club soda. Crush the sugar with a wooden muddler, chopstick, strong spoon, lipstick, or cartridge case, whatever. Rotate the glass so that the sugar grains and bitters give it a lining. Add a large ice cube. Pour in the rye (or bourbon). Serve with a stirring rod.

CONTINUED FROM

THE **FOOLPROOF** DAIQUIRI

ONE MAN'S (RATHER PUSHY) TECHINIQUE FOR ASSURING THE PERFECT DRINK EVERY TIME

By John Mariani

SINCE THERE ARE ONLY ABOUT a half-dozen true bartenders left in the world, with the rest barely capable of making anything other than vodka martinis, I decided that the only way I'd ever get a classic daiquiri, straight up, was to have the recipe printed on the back of my business card so I could hand it to the person behind the bar who might otherwise make it with strawberries or bananas, on the rocks or frozen.

Ever since I had the cards done, with a picture of the cocktail glass I want it served in, I've been getting exactly the daiquiri named after the Cuban town of Daiquiri, where, after the Spanish-American War,

Americans came to run the mines, spending off-hours drinking local rum with local lime juice and local sugar.

F. Scott Fitzgerald was the first to mention it in print, in *This Side of Paradise* (1920), and Hemingway—who drank his daiquiris without sugar—wrote of the cocktail, "The frappéd part of the drink was like the wake of a ship and the clear part was the way the water looked when the bow cut it when you were in shallow water over marl bottom. That was almost the exact color."

A drink so perfect demands respect. And knowledge. So I have my cards.

DAIQUIRI

SERVES 1

GLASS TYPE: COCKTAIL GLASS

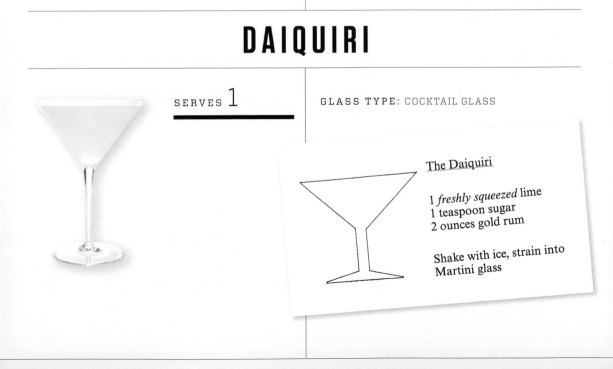

The Daiquiri

1 *freshly squeezed* lime
1 teaspoon sugar
2 ounces gold rum

Shake with ice, strain into Martini glass

The
FIVE-MINUTE GUIDE TO OYSTERS

By Francine Maroukian

Despite its perfectly reasonable desire to protect its fleshy treasure, an oyster is nothing short of shuckable in the right hands. Just coax apart the shell and the oyster presents itself, damp and salty, resting in a pool of its own briny nectar ("liquor") and smelling delicately of the water that bore it. An oyster's flavor and texture are a direct result of the mineral content, salinity, and temperature of the gallons of water it filters through its gills every hour, which is why different origins create very different tastes. The next time your fishmonger reels off a list of the day's offerings, let this be your guide.

FOUR THINGS YOU SHOULD KNOW ABOUT OYSTERS

Learn more about this tasty (and provocative) bivalve.

1. Oysters, found in estuaries where seawater mixes with freshwater, are shelled invertebrates (or cold-blooded, soft-bodied animals without backbones, like snails) classified as bivalves. While oysters have separate sexes, they may change sex one or more times during their life span, and there is no way of telling by examining their shells.

2. It isn't as relevant with today's cultivated oysters, but warm-water months without an *r* (May, June, July, and August) traditionally make up the spawning season, during which oysters tend to be thinner and less tasty, as energy is directed to reproduction. (The heat during these summer months also impacts safety and shipping.)

3. An oyster holds itself together with about 22 pounds of pressure (for protection and to prevent dehydrating during low tide). The more frequently an oyster opens, the stronger the muscle and the tighter the seal, producing a better shelf life when it leaves the water.

4. When Aphrodite bestowed her aphrodisiacal qualities on oysters, it was more than myth. In addition to their provocative appearance, oysters are loaded with zinc (which controls progesterone levels, linked to increased libido), iron, and other stamina-inducing nutrients.

THE EAST COAST–WEST COAST OYSTER FEUD

Atlantic and Pacific coasts certainly have their differences.

Native East Coast oysters are all the same species—grown subtidally with smooth shells—and are typically sold under regional names like Wellfleets (from Cape Cod), Blue Points (Long Island), Chincoteagues (Virginia), and Apalachicolas (Florida). Eastern oysters tend to be milder than those farmed from the West Coast, although their taste and texture vary with location. The cold-water temperatures of New England slow down metabolism, producing slightly crisp, sweeter oysters; expect meatier, flabbier oysters with more saltiness as you work your way down the coast into warmer waters.

The only species native to the Pacific Northwest is the tiny Olympia, named after the once-thriving oyster community in Washington's Puget Sound and a casualty of shoreline pollution and overfishing (particularly during the California Gold Rush). The Olympia is making a slow comeback, and its silver-dollar size and clean, almost cucumberlike finish make it a perfect cocktail oyster.

As the Olympia went into near extinction, exotic varieties were imported from Japan: the Pacific oyster, found from southeastern Alaska to Baja, California, and later, the less prevalent Kumamoto. Both are typically grown intertidally and have rough, fluted shells. The Kumamoto oyster has plump meat with a sweet, subtle mineral flavor that is perfect for half-shell beginners. There are many regional varieties of Pacific oysters, ranging from slightly fruity with a green-apple finish to crisp and lightly salty to full-on briny with a sublime steely aftertaste.

HOW TO SHUCK AN OYSTER

Keep your fingers safe: John Finger from Hog Island Oyster teaches you how to unlock the magic of the oyster without injuring yourself.

Shucking can be dangerous, and as speed and numbers increase, so does the risk—hence the chain-mail gloves made just for this task. But Finger brings it simply and safely down to four steps. All you need is a clean, dry kitchen towel, a good oyster knife (below), and a modicum of good sense.

THE EQUIPMENT YOU'LL NEED

The Dish: Serving oysters on a bed of crushed ice not only keeps them cold, it keeps them level, so you don't lose any of the nectar. Traditional French-style 14-inch stainless steel oyster platter, $18, and stand, $12, plus shipping; 800-473-0577; jbprince.com

The Knife: We recommend a 4-inch Dexter-Russell with a stain-free, high-carbon-steel blade and a polypropylene handle for a slip-resistant grip. $15, plus shipping; 415-663-9218; hogislandoysters.com

---

STEP ONE

Under cold running water, scrub any mud or dirt from the shell (it should be tightly closed and feel heavy) with a stiff wire brush. Keep the oysters refrigerated (cup-side down to help retain their nectar) and covered with a damp, clean kitchen towel until ready to serve.

STEP TWO

Using a folded towel or glove, securely hold the oyster cup side down with the point (or hinge side) toward you. Keep your hand across the oyster, perpendicular to the knife. Insert the oyster knife through the hinge, angling the blade down into the cup of the oyster. When you feel the knife sink in, twist it as if you were turning an ignition key until you hear the hinge pop.

STEP THREE

Starting at the adductor muscle—the tough little band that clamps the two sides of the shell together—scrape the blade across the top of the shell (similar to keeping the knife near the bone when filleting fish) by rotating the oyster until the adductor muscle is on the far side of the shell, away from you. (When you open the oyster, there shouldn't be any meat attached to the top shell.)

STEP FOUR

Rotate the oyster so the adductor muscle is now directly in front of you again, sliding the knife under the muscle to loosen the meat. Check for any shell or grit. Settle the bottom of each shell into a bed of crushed ice and serve immediately.

BIVALVES AT YOUR DOORSTEP

WEST COAST: THE HOG BOX FROM HOG ISLAND OYSTER COMPANY

Three dozen Sweetwaters—lightly salty with a smoky-sweet flavor and a long, oval-shaped, fluted shell—packed with a glove, knife, and Hog Island T-shirt and hat. $90, plus shipping and handling; 415-663-9218; hogislandoysters.com

EAST COAST: MAC'S SEAFOOD

Direct from the salty waters of Cape Cod Bay, Massachusetts's long, strong-shelled oysters have slightly crisp flesh with a flinty "cold water" taste. One dozen Wellfleets packed with a knife and Mac's tangy cocktail sauce. $49, plus shipping and handling; macsseafood.com

THREE THINGS TO EAT
AT COCKTAIL HOUR

(ESPECIALLY IF THERE IS VODKA IN THE COCKTAILS)

By Ryan Poli

CHEF, PERENNIAL, CHICAGO

I GREW UP ON THE SOUTH SIDE OF CHICAGO, by Midway Airport. The neighborhood was predominantly Polish and Italian, with a lot of Eastern Europeans—a strange mix, but everyone liked food. My first restaurant job was at a place called the Candlelight. Around the holidays, Kristina, a huge, strong woman from Poland, would make a spread of what she called *zakuski*—things like eel with aspic, headcheese, a lot of caviar. I was seventeen. There was no way I was eating that stuff. Then the chef, Mike, forced me to eat some caviar on a potato pancake, and that was the beginning for me and Russian food. These three *zakuski* go great with vodka. (Of course, vodka goes with anything.) I think the Candlelight is a Krispy Kreme now.

Crab with Potatoes and Dill

SERVES 4 TO 6

DIFFICULTY:

6 small red potatoes

coarse salt and freshly ground black pepper

4 oz fresh crabmeat, picked over

2 sprigs fresh dill, chopped

¼ tsp grated lemon zest

1 to 2 tbsp mayonnaise

canola oil

sherry vinegar

paprika for garnish

- Buy potatoes that are all roughly the same size—this will help them cook evenly and it looks better when you serve them. Wash the potatoes in cold water and pat dry. Cut each in half, then slice off the bottom of each so it has a base to stand on without wobbling around. Using a melon baller, scoop out the center of each potato half, leaving a little crater for the crab to sit in. Put the potatoes in a pot and cover with cold water with a few pinches of salt. Simmer—do not boil—until the potatoes are tender. It's important not to overcook them—when cooled they should still have some snap when you bite in. Start checking after 5 minutes. Chill and reserve until later.

- Mix the crabmeat with the dill, salt, pepper, lemon zest, and mayo—not too much, as you don't want to mask the flavor of the crab. Taste the crab to make sure it has enough flavor.

- To finish, toss the potatoes with a little salt, canola oil, and sherry vinegar—just a few drops of each. Spoon some crab mixture into each potato, dividing it evenly among the 12 halves. Sprinkle each with a little paprika, and serve.

Russian Beet Salad with Orange and Walnuts

SERVES 4

DIFFICULTY:

EASY | REASONABLE | WORTH THE EFFORT

3 or 4 large red beets

2 oranges

about ½ cup walnuts

coarse salt and freshly ground black pepper

1 tbsp canola oil

sherry vinegar

- Preheat the oven to 350°F. Cover the beets (you can use jarred beets instead of cooking them fresh, but make sure they're good quality) with cold water, place over high heat, and simmer until tender enough to be pierced by a paring knife. (This will take up to 12 minutes of simmering. After 8 minutes, start checking. If they're still hard, cook longer.) Remove and let cool. Peel the beets with your fingers, cut into cubes, and set aside.

- Using a sharp knife, cut away the peel of the oranges; leaving no peel or white pith. Try cutting between the lines of the orange to make segments, but if you have trouble, no worries—just cut slices.

- Toast a handful of walnuts on a baking sheet in the preheated oven for about 3 minutes, then cool.

- TO ASSEMBLE: Toss the beets with a pinch each of salt and pepper, the oil, and a few drops of sherry vinegar. Taste the beets. If they need more salt or vinegar, add a little more. Put the beets in a bowl, with the oranges and walnuts on top.

CONTINUED

Pickled Mushrooms on Russian Black Toast with Garlic

SERVES 4 TO 6

DIFFICULTY:

EASY **REASONABLE** WORTH THE EFFORT

1 to 1½ lb mushrooms

½ small onion

2 cloves garlic, plus 1 halved clove for the toast

2 sprigs fresh thyme

2 sprigs fresh tarragon

large pinch of black peppercorns

large pinch of whole allspice

2 whole cloves

2 cups red wine vinegar

1 cup sugar

coarse salt

4 to 6 slices Russian black bread (or pumpernickel)

olive oil for drizzling

2 tbsp minced fresh flat-leaf parsley

- Thoroughly wash whatever wild mushrooms are available (a great combination would be chanterelle, lobster, morel, but also delicious, and easier to find, would be portobello, cremini, oyster). Trim the stems and coarsely dice the mushrooms. Tie in a cheesecloth square: the onion, garlic, thyme, tarragon, peppercorns, allspice, and the cloves. Put in a saucepan along with the vinegar, 1 cup water, the sugar, and a couple pinches of salt. Bring everything to a boil, add the mushrooms, turn down the heat, and simmer for about 10 minutes. Turn off the heat and let the mushrooms cool in the liquid, then remove the mushrooms and discard the rest.

- Toast a few slices of Russian black bread (or pumpernickel). Rub each slice with the cut side of the garlic, drizzle with olive oil, and sprinkle with the parsley.

- To serve, take the mushrooms out of the liquid and place in a serving bowl, sprinkle with salt, and serve with the toasted bread around the bowl.

 CONTINUED FROM

ESQUIRE
Classics

PRETTY EASY RECIPES FOR SOME OF THE BEST COCKTAIL SNACKS OF ALL TIME.

Reprinted from the *Esquire Cookbook*, 1955

NUTS

Crunchy and appetite-provoking.

Toss English walnut meats into a skillet with a little bubbling butter, stir, and brown delicately. When nearly done, sprinkle generously with salt, and dust not too liberally with chili powder. Turn out on paper towels for a few moments, until the excess fat is absorbed.

Blanch almonds and place in sizzling butter with a mashed clove of garlic. Turn and stir for 15 minutes, when the nuts should be nicely tanned. Sprinkle with salt; place on paper towels to drain.

Toss ½ pound of shelled walnuts into a frying pan with a goodly piece of butter. Let them brown as you stir, then salt to taste, dust with curry powder, and drain on paper towels.

P.M. SCRAMBLED EGGS

You know how to make plain scrambled eggs of the breakfast variety; here's how to perk them up for the midnight snack. For each egg, use 1 tablespoon cream, 1 teaspoon crumbled Roquefort cheese, a dash of Worcestershire sauce, a pinch of powdered tarragon, salt, and pepper. Beat together lightly. Have frying pan very hot, let butter sizzle in it, pour in eggs, allow to set slightly, stir with a fork, and turn off the heat. Toast and butter slice of white bread. Give eggs a final stir—don't overcook! Heap on toast. Some orange marmalade, picnic sausages delicately browned, a pot of coffee.

HOT STUFFED MUSHROOMS

Use large mushrooms. Peel caps, remove and chop stems, then sauté caps in butter about 15 minutes. Chop leftover lobster or crab meat with a modest bit of garlic. Add a few drops of Worcestershire sauce, the minced stems of mushrooms, a beaten egg, and a little salt. Heap caps with this mixture, sprinkle with bread crumbs, brush with melted butter, and put into moderate oven for 15 minutes. Spear with toothpicks and serve hot.

CRUSHED OLIVES

As made by Sal Cucinotta of Teddy's Restaurant, New York.

Spread a cloth over a cutting board and crush Sicilian-type green olives, four at a time, with the base of a soft-drink bottle. Remove pits; squeeze crushed olives in the hands until brine is removed. Two pounds of olives does it for a large, hungry crowd. Make a dressing of 1 cup imported olive oil, black pepper to taste, 2 cloves of finely chopped garlic, ½ teaspoon oregano, 1 medium Bermuda onion cut in paper-thin slices, 2 stalks crisp celery cut in 1-inch pieces. Add the olives and 2 bay leaves, sprinkle with chopped fresh parsley, and refrigerate. Let the cocktails be dusty-dry and dip into the appetizer with your fingers.

MINIATURE PIZZAS

Mix some tomato paste with grated onion to taste and some chopped anchovies. Spread thick on split English muffins. Dust with grated Italian cheese (Parmesan or Romano). Toast in oven until muffins are lightly browned and topping is bubbling. Cut into tiny wedges, serve hot with cocktails.

Or drain a can of tomatoes. Season the pulp with crushed garlic, grated onion, salt, and pepper. Spoon onto split English muffins. Top with thin slices of mozzarella cheese. Toast in oven until cheese is melted and bubbling.

THINGS A MAN SHOULD KNOW ABOUT
CHEESE

By Anne Saxelby

Most people don't think of it this way, but cheese is alive. Like wine, it has a kind of flavor curve as it ages. You open a bottle of wine, you drink it. Same when you cut into a wheel of cheese—ideally, it should get sold and eaten within a few days.

Bread. Not crackers. If anything with it at all.

When you buy a slice of prepacked cheese, you have no idea how long it's been sitting there in that asphyxiating plastic wrap. Plus, the plastic wrap actually interacts in a noxious way with the fats in the cheese, leading to refrigerator taste.

I'm not sure what would possess someone to buy pregrated cheese.

You don't need to spend a lot of money on cheese. But be aware that there is a vast range of quality out there. True, handmade farmstead cheeses will always cost more. They will also taste incredibly better and more complex than their industrial counterparts.

I guess crackers are okay. It just seems a little like propping the *Mona Lisa* up against the dresser in your bedroom.

To prepare a cheese plate of which you can be proud: Buy three to five cheeses. Look for a variety of styles, textures, and kinds of milks (cow, sheep, goat). Try picking three of these: One soft and creamy, like a fresh goat or Brie-like cheese; one well-aged firm cheese; one blue; one super-pungent cheese.

But really, just buy what you like. Unless of course your date likes something you find disgusting. This is what's known as love.

A note on order: Begin with the mild cheeses, and pro-gress to strong ones. If you gobble up all blue cheese first, it's like a punch in the teeth to your palate. So much salt! So much flavor! After that, it makes it harder to taste the other ones.

Find a good cheese shop. People who work behind cheese counters are usually obsessed and can help you navigate the case. Short of that, Whole Foods is a decent option.

You can eat cheese all by itself. You don't actually need other fancy stuff. That's how they've been doing it in France for hundreds of years.

That said, it can be delicious to pair fancy stuff with your cheese to see how the flavors interact. Sweet foods like honey, preserves, or dried fruit seem to work exceptionally well with strong cheeses, especially blues. On the savory side, roasted nuts, charcuterie, pickles, chutneys, and mustards can also be good cheese-plate accessories.

Before or after dinner? Always a good question. Europeans eat a cheese course after the salad but before dessert. And someone once told me it's been scientifically proven that ending your meal with a basic food like cheese actually aids in digestion. I love when I can use science as an excuse to eat more cheese.

But we do live in America, and cheese before dinner makes a delicious appetizer. Not too much—you want to be sure your date gets to savor the rest of your culinary skills.

Cheese is best at room temperature. When it's cold, some of the flavors can kind of go dormant. When you let it sit for a bit, the flavors come out and the texture improves too.

Wrap in waxed paper, put it in a zip-top bag, store it in the fridge.

If you don't have zip-top bags, waxed paper and then aluminum foil works too. The main thing is, you don't want the cut face of the cheese to touch plastic or foil.

If you don't have any waxed paper or foil, just eat the cheese.

The basic rule is: Soft cheeses—your goat cheeses, your mozzarellas, your Brie-style cheeses—need to be eaten sooner than hard cheeses. Within five days of opening. Hard ones like Parmigiano-Reggiano, Comté, Cheddars, and aged Goudas have less moisture, so they keep forever. (Trim the mold off the surface.) I once bought an ambitious chunk of Parmigiano that took me seven months to finish.

I sometimes get asked to put together a cheese plate when the only store for miles is a big, boxy supermarket. Turns out there are decent options. Hard cheeses like Parmigiano and Manchego are readily available across the States, and pretty reliable quality-wise. Aged Gouda-style cheeses like Prima Donna and Rembrandt are also a safe bet. You can usually find a log of fresh goat cheese, which you can dress up with honey or freshly chopped herbs. Bries and other soft-ripened cheeses are generally lackluster but can be palatable when you do sinful things to them, like baking them in pastry crust.

And most supermarkets also seem to have a variety of blue cheeses for the nibbling. I steer toward Italian ones like Gorgonzola and away from the Danish blue. Grandpas have an affinity for it, but that stuff could take the paint off a car.

Yellow Cheddar is yellow because of annatto seed, a natural dye that's been used in Cheddar for a long time. I don't know why. Ever drink orange milk?

Cheese is seasonal. Most dairy animals breed in the fall, are pregnant and chilling out in the barn all winter long, and give birth in the spring. And like humans, a cow, goat, or sheep has to have a baby in order to make milk. The milking begins in the spring and winds up in the late fall or early winter. That means that we're genetically tuned to eat fresh cheeses in the springtime, a whole variety of fresh and aged cheeses in the summer and fall, and hearty, robust aged cheeses in the winter.

That said, most dairies nowadays don't operate that way. But it does make sense that in the summer months we want light, tangy cheeses like mozzarella or feta or fresh goat cheese, and in the winter we want to feast on dense, rich cheeses like Comté.

White wines are ideal with cheese. Reds can be great but tend to have bold flavors and sometimes drown out the siren song of a little piece o' cheese. So: Pouilly-Fussé, chardonnay, sauvignon blanc. Rieslings are great, provided they aren't too sweet. I love a bit of bubbly with light, fresh cheeses, and can get down with some crisp Italian whites like Verdicchio or Vermentino. On the red side, a basic Côtes du Rhône or pinot noir always seems to do the trick, though my favorites are brighter and fruitier Italians like montepulciano, dolcetto, and barbera. Of course, a good craft beer and a good cheese is a match made in heaven.

And sweet dessert wines like port, sherry, and Sauternes can be incredibly delicious.

I've also been known to try whiskey, bourbon, mead, cider . . . you name it. Basically, if it's fermented, I'm going to try to pair it with cheese.

For grilled cheese sandwiches: You want a cheese that's going to melt nicely and not get all oily and weird, or stay like a slab of marble on top of your bread. Most Cheddars, fontinas, and Gruyère-style cheeses work well. If you're not sure which ones those are, ask your cheesemonger.

I love being called a cheesemonger.

Anne Saxelby is the owner of Saxelby Cheesemongers in New York City.

A LIST OF **THE CHEFS** IN THIS BOOK

HUGH ACHESON

Empire State South
Atlanta, GA
404-541-1105
empirestatesouth.com

Five and Ten
Athens, GA
706-546-7300
fiveandten.com

The National
Athens, GA
706-549-3450
thenationalrestaurant.com

PAUL BARTOLOTTA

Bacchus
Milwaukee, WI
414-765-1166
bacchusmke.com

Bartolotta's Lake Park Bistro
Milwaukee, WI
414-962-6300
lakeparkbistro.com

Bartolotta Ristorante di Mare
Las Vegas, NV
702-248-3463
wynnlasvegas.com

Harbor House
Milwaukee, WI
414-395-4900
harborhousemke.com

Mr. B's
Brookfield, WI
262-790-7005
mrbssteakhouse.com

Pizzeria Piccola
Wauwatosa, WI
414-443-0800
pizzeriapiccola.com

Ristorante Bartolotta
Wauwatosa, WI
414-771-7910
bartolottaristorante.com

MARIO BATALI

B&B Ristorante
Las Vegas, NV
702-266-9977
bandbristorante.com

Babbo
New York, NY
212-777-0303
babbonyc.com

Carnevino Italian Steakhouse
Las Vegas, NV
702-789-4141
carnevino.com

Casa Mono and Bar Jamón
New York, NY
212-253-2773
casamononyc.com

Del Posto
New York, NY
212-497-8090
delposto.com

Eataly
New York, NY
212-229-2560
mariobatali.com/
restaurants_eataly.cfm

Esca
New York, NY
212-564-7272
esca-nyc.com

Lupa
New York, NY
212-982-5089
luparestaurant.com

Osteria Mozza
Los Angeles, CA
323-297-0100
mozza-la.com

OTTO Enoteca Pizzeria
New York, NY
212-995-9559
Las Vegas, NV
702-677-3390
ottopizzeria.com

Pizzeria Mozza
Los Angeles, CA
323-297-0101
mozz-la.com

Spotted Pig
New York, NY
212-620-0393
spottedpig.com

Tarry Lodge
Port Chester, NY
914-939-3111
tarrylodge.com

ZACH BELL

Café Boulud Palm Beach
Palm Beach, FL
561-655-6060
danielnyc.com

JOHN BESH

The American Sector
New Orleans, LA
504-528-1940
nationalww2museum.org

August
New Orleans, LA
504-299-9777
restaurantaugust.com

Besh Steak
New Orleans, LA
504-533-6111
harrahsneworleans.com

Domenica
New Orleans, LA
504-648-6020
domenicarestaurant.com

La Provence
Lacombe, LA
985-626-7662
laprovencerestaurant.com

Lüke
New Orleans, LA
504-378-2840
lukeneworleans.com

BRIAN BISTRONG

Braeburn
New York, NY
212-255-0696
braeburnrestaurant.com

DANIEL BOULUD

Bar Boulud
New York, NY
212-595-0303
danielnyc.com

Bar Pleiades
New York, NY
212-772-2600
danielnyc.com

Café Boulud Palm Beach
Palm Beach, FL
561-655-6060
danielnyc.com

Daniel
New York, NY
212-288-0033
danielnyc.com

DB Bistro Moderne
New York, NY
212-391-2400
Miami, FL
305-350-0750
danielnyc.com

DBGB Kitchen & Bar
New York, NY
212-933-5300
danielnyc.com

JIMMY BRADLEY

The Harrison
New York, NY
212-274-9310
theharrison.com

The Red Cat
New York, NY
212-242-1122
theredcat.com

SEAN BROCK

Husk
Charleston, SC
843-577-2500
huskrestaurant.com

McCrady's
Charleston, SC
843-577-0025
mccradysrestaurant.com

DAVID BULL

Bar Congress
Austin, TX
512-827-2755
congressaustin.com

Congress
Austin, TX
512-827-2760
congressaustin.com

Second Bar + Kitchen
Austin, TX
512-827-2750
congressaustin.com

JOEY CAMPANARO

Kenmare
New York, NY
212-274-9898
kenmarenyc.com

The Little Owl
New York, NY
212-741-4695
thelittleowlnyc.com

Market Table
New York, NY
212-255-2100
markettablenyc.com

MARCO CANORA

Hearth
New York, NY
646-602-1300
restauranthearth.com

Terroir
New York, NY
(East Village)
212-602-1300
New York, NY
(Tribeca)
212-625-9463
wineisterroir.com

ANDREW CARMELLINI

The Dutch
New York, NY
212-677-6200
andrewcarmellini.com

Locanda Verde
New York, NY
212-925-3797
locandaverdenyc.com

BRYAN CASWELL

Little Bigs
Houston, TX
713-521-2447
littlebigshouston.com

Reef
Houston, TX
713-526-8282
reefhouston.com

Stella Sola
Houston, TX
713-880-1001
stellasolahouston.com

DAVID CHANG

Má Pêche
New York, NY
212-757-5878
momofuku.com/ma-peche

Momofuku Ko
New York, NY
212-500-0831
momofuku.com/ko

Momofuku Milk Bar
New York, NY
212-757-5878
momofuku.com/milk-bar

Momofuku Noodle Bar
New York, NY
212-777-7773
momofuku.com/noodle-bar

Momofuku Ssäm Bar
New York, NY
212-254-3500
momofuku.com/ssam-bar

RAYMOND CHEN

Inn at West View Farm
Dorset, VT
800-769-4903
www.innatwestviewfarm
.com

AMANDA COHEN

Dirt Candy
New York, NY
212-228-7732
dirtcandynyc.com

TOM COLICCHIO

Colicchio & Sons
New York, NY
212.400.6699
colicchioandsons.com

craft
Atlanta, GA
404-995-7580
Dallas, TX
214-397-4111
Los Angeles, CA
310-279-4180
craftrestaurant.com

craftbar
Atlanta, GA
404-995-7580
Los Angeles, CA
310-279-4180
New York, NY
212-461-4300
craftrestaurant.com

craftsteak
Las Vegas, NV
702-891-7318
Mashantucket, CT
860-312-7272
craftrestaurant.com

'wichcraft
Las Vegas, NV
702-891-3166
New York, NY
212-780-0577
San Francisco, CA
415-593-3895
wichcraftnyc.com

SCOTT CONANT

Faustina
New York, NY
212-475-3400
scottconant.com

Scarpetta
Beverly Hills, CA
310-860-7970
Las Vegas, NV
702-698-7000
Miami Beach, FL
305-538-2000,
305-674-4660
New York, NY
212-691-0555
scottconant.com

FRANK CRISPO

Crispo
New York, NY
212-229-1818
crisporestaurant.com

JOHN CURRENCE

City Grocery
Oxford, MS
662-232-8080
citygroceryonline.com

KEVIN DAVIS

Steelhead Diner
Seattle, WA
206-625-0129
steelheaddiner.com

HAROLD DIETERLE

Perilla
New York, NY
212-929-6868
perillanyc.com

Kin Shop
New York, NY
212-675-4295
kinshopnyc.com

WYLIE DUFRESNE

wd-50
New York, NY
212-477-2900
wd-50.com

ROB EVANS

Duckfat
Portland, ME
207-774-8080
duckfat.com

Hugo's
Portland, ME
207-774-8538
hugos.net

EVAN FUNKE

Rustic Canyon
Santa Monica, CA
310-393-7050
rusticcanyonwinebar.com

MARK GAIER and CLARK FRASIER

Arrows
Ogunquit, ME
207-361-1100
arrowsrestaurant.com

MC Perkins Cove
Ogunquit, ME
207-646-6263 ext 1
mcperkinscove.com

Summer Winter
Burlington, MA
781-221-6643
summerwinterrestaurant
.com

SUZANNE GOIN

A.O.C. Wine Bar
Los Angeles, CA
323-653-6359
aocwinebar.com

Lucques
Los Angeles, CA
323-655-6277
lucques.com

Tavern
Los Angeles, CA
310-806-6464
tavernla.com

BILLY GRANT

Bricco Trattoria
Glastonbury, CT
860-659-0220
billygrant.com

Grants
West Hartford, CT
860-236-1930
billygrant.com

Restaurant Bricco
West Hartford, CT
860-233-0220
billygrant.com

KOREN GRIEVESON

Avec
Chicago, IL
312-377-2002
avecrestaurant.com

STEPHANIE HARRIS

The Island Inn
Monhegan Island, ME
207-596-0371
islandinnmonhegan.com

EMMA HEARST

Sorella
New York, NY
212-274-9595
sorellanyc.com

LEE HEFTER

Cut Beverly Hills
Beverly Hills, CA
310-276-8500
wolfgangpuck.com

Spago Beverly Hills
Beverly Hills, CA
310-276-8500
wolfgangpuck.com

WP24
Los Angeles, CA
213-743-8824
wolfgangpuck.com

MATT HILL

Charlie Palmer Steak
Washington, DC
202-547-8100
charliepalmer.com

LINTON HOPKINS

Holeman & Finch Public House
Atlanta, GA
404-948-1175
holeman-finch.com

Restaurant Eugene
Atlanta, GA
404-355-0321
restauranteugene.com

DAVID KATZ

Mémé
Philadelphia, PA
215-735-4900
memerestaurant.com

DOUGLAS KEANE

Cyrus
Healdsburg, CA
707-433-3311
cyrusrestaurant.com

THOMAS KELLER

Ad Hoc
Yountville, CA
707-944-2487
adhocrestaurant.com

Bouchon
Beverly Hills, CA
310-271-9910
Las Vegas, NV
702-414-6200
Yountville, CA
707-944-8037
bouchonbistro.com

Bouchon Bakery
Las Vegas, NV
702-414-6203
Yountville, CA
707-944-2253
bouchonbakery.com

The French Laundry
Yountville, CA
707-944-2380
frenchlaundry.com

Per Se
New York, NY
212-823-9335
perseny.com

DENNIS LEARY

Canteen
San Francisco, CA
415-928-8870
sfcanteen.com

Golden West
San Francisco, CA
415-392-3246
theauwest.com

The Sentinel
San Francisco, CA
415-284-9960
thesentinelsf.com

EDWARD LEE

610 Magnolia
Louisville, KY
502-636-0783
610magnolia.com

PETER McANDREWS

Modo Mio
Philadelphia, PA
215-203-8707
modomiorestaurant.com

Paesano's
Philadelphia, PA
(West Girard Avenue)
267-886-9556
Philadelphia, PA

(Italian Market)
215-922-2220
paesanosphillystyle.com

SHAWN McCLAIN

Custom House Tavern
Chicago, IL
312-523-0200
customhouse.cc

Green Zebra
Chicago, IL
312-243-7100
greenzebrachicago.com

Spring
Chicago, IL
773-395-7100
springrestaurant.net

MICHAEL MINA*

American Fish
Las Vegas, NV
702-590-8610

Arcadia
San Jose, CA
408-278-4555

Bourbon Steak
Detroit, MI
313-465-1734
Miami, FL
786-279-6600
San Francisco, CA
415-397-3003
Scottsdale, AZ
480-513-6002
Washington, DC
202-944-2026

Clock Bar
San Francisco, CA
415-397-9222

Michael Mina
Las Vegas, NV
702-693-7223
San Francisco, CA
415-397-9222

Nobhill Tavern
Las Vegas, NV
702-891-7337

RN74
San Francisco, CA
415-543-7474

Saltwater
Detroit, MI
313-465-1646

Seablue
Atlantic City, NJ
609-317-8220
Las Vegas, NV
702-891-7433

Stonehill Tavern
Dana Point, CA
949-234-3318

Stripsteak
Las Vegas, NV
702-632-7414

XIV
Los Angeles, CA
323-656-1414

*For all Michael
Mina restaurants,
see michaelmina.net*

RICK MOONEN

RM Seafood at Mandalay Bay
Las Vegas, NV
702-632-9300
rmseafood.com

DAVID MYERS

Comme Ça
Las Vegas, NV
877-551-7776
cosmopolitanlasvegas.com

Comme Ça
West Hollywood, CA
323-782-1104
commecarestaurant.com

Pizzeria Ortica
Costa Mesa, CA
714-445-4900
pizzeriaortica.com

Sona
Los Angeles, CA
310-659-7708
sonarestaurant.com

LUKE PALLADINO

Luke Palladino Seasonal Italian Cooking
Northfield, NJ
609-646-8189
lukepalladino.com

CHARLIE PALMER*

Astra
New York, NY
212-644-9394

Aureole
Las Vegas, NV
702-632-7401
New York, NY
212-319-1660

Briscola
Reno, NV
775-789-2587

Charlie Palmer at Bloomingdale's South Coast Plaza
Costa Mesa, CA
714-352-2525

Charlie Palmer Steak
Las Vegas, NV
702-632-5120
Reno, NV
775-789-2458
Washington, DC
202-547-8100

Dry Creek Kitchen
Healdsburg, CA
707-431-0330

Fin Fish
Reno, NV
775-789-2456

Métrazur
New York, NY
212-687-4600

For all Charlie Palmer restaurants, see charliepalmer.com

MATHIEU PALOMBINO

Motorino
Brooklyn, NY
718-599-8899
New York, NY
212-777-2644
motorinopizza.com

CHRIS PANDEL

The Bristol
Chicago, IL
773-862-5555
thebristolchicago.com

DAVE PASTERNACK

Esca
New York, NY
212-564-7272
esca-nyc.com

SCOTT PEACOCK

Chef and cookbook author

ZAKARY PELACCIO

5 Ninth
New York, NY
212-929-9460
5ninth.com

Fatty Crab
New York, NY
(Upper West Side)
212-496-2722

New York, NY
(West Village)
212-352-3592
fattycrab.com

Fatty 'Cue
Brooklyn, NY
718-599-3090
fattycue.com

RIA PELL

Ria's Bluebird
Atlanta, GA
404-521-3737
riasbluebird.com

Sauced
Atlanta, GA
404-688-6553
saucedatlanta.com

STEVEN PETRECCA

Jones
Philadelphia, PA
215-223-5663
jones-restaurant.com

RYAN POLI

Perennial
Chicago, IL
312-381-7070
perennialchicago.com

LEE RICHARDSON

Ashley's
Little Rock, AR
501-374-7474
capitalhotel.com

ERIC RIPERT

10 Arts Bistro & Lounge
Philadelphia, PA
215-523-8273
10arts.com

Blue by Eric Ripert
Grand Cayman,
Cayman Islands
345-943-9000
ritzcarlton.com

Le Bernardin
New York, NY
212-554-1515
le-bernardin.com

Westend Bistro
Washington, DC
202-974-4914
westendbistrodc.com

BILL RODGERS

Keens Steakhouse
New York, NY
212-947-3636
keens.com

BARTON SEAVER

bartonseaver.org

KERRY SIMON

Simon at Palms Place
Las Vegas, NV
702-944-3292
simonatpalmsplace.com

Simon LA
Los Angeles, CA
310-358-3979
simonlarestaurant.com

MICHAEL SYMON

Bar Symon
Avon Lake, OH
440-933-5652
barsymon.com

BSpot Burgers
Woodmere, OH
216-292-5567
bspotburgers.com

Lola
Cleveland, OH
216-621-5652
lolabistro.com

Lolita
Tremont, OH
216-771-5652
lolabistro.com

Roast
Detroit, MI
313-961-2500
roastdetroit.com

JET TILA

Wazuzu
Las Vegas, NV
702-770-5388
www.encorelasvegas.com

BRYAN VOLTAGGIO

Volt
Frederick, MD
301-696-8658
voltrestaurant.com

WOLFGANG VOMEND

Bavarian Inn
Shepherdstown, WV
304-876-2551
bavarianinnwv.com

DAVID WALTUCK

Former chef and owner of Chanterelle in New York City

DAVE WALZOG

Lakeside Grill
Las Vegas, NV
702-770-9966
wynnlasvegas.com

SW Steakhouse
Las Vegas, NV
702-248-3463
wynnlasvegas.com

MICHAEL WHITE

Alto
New York, NY
212-308-1099
altorestaurant.com

Convivio
New York, NY
212-599-5045
convivionyc.com

Due Mari
New Brunswick, NJ
732-296-1600
duemarinj.com/index.html

Due Terre
Bernardsville, NJ
908-221-0040
dueterre.com

Marea
New York, NY
212-582-5100
marea-nyc.com

Osteria Morini
New York, NY
212-965-8777
osteriamorini.com

SUE ZEMANICK

Gautreau's
New Orleans, LA
504-899-7397
gautreausrestaurant.com

RANDY ZWEIBAN

Province
Chicago, IL
213-669-9900
provincerestaurant.com

THE RECIPES BY SKILL LEVEL

A COMPLETE LIST, IN ORDER OF DIFFICULTY

EASY

REASONABLE

WORTH THE EFFORT

INDEX

Credits

Acknowledgments

ESQUIRE **WOULD LIKE TO THANK** the following people for making this cookbook into a cookbook:

- **FRANCINE MAROUKIAN:** "Acknowledgment" is too weak a word. For more than a decade, Francine has contributed her unparalleled, unimpeachable culinary knowledge, wisdom, and soul to the pages of *Esquire* magazine. Finding and telling the world about interesting and wonderful food makes her truly happy—she loves it, and we have tried to translate her love into this volume. Quite literally, the book would not exist without her.

- **THE CHEFS:** Every chef in this book worked hard to create a perfect recipe for us—for you—and we thank them for their generosity in allowing us to present a little of their talent, personality, and expertise. We feel this book contains an epic collection of recipes, and it all came from their heads.

- **THE WRITERS** whose work makes this book indispensable by inspiring us all to get into the kitchen, think about what we're doing, and enjoy the results: Ted Allen, Tom Chiarella, Cal Fussman, Tom Junod, John Mariani, Ross McCammon, Scott Raab, Mike Sager, and David Wondrich. Also, Tom Colicchio, for the rousing foreword.

- **THE PEOPLE BEHIND THIS BOOK:** Charlie Melcher, Lauren Nathan, and Lia Ronnen at Melcher Media; Lorena Jones at Chronicle Books; Jacqueline Deval at Hearst Books; Paul Kepple, Ralph Geroni, and Susan Van Horn at Headcase Design; and, at *Esquire*, Peter Griffin, David Curcurito, John Kenney, Michael Norseng, Alison Unterreiner, Whitney Tressel, Kevin McDonnell, Soni Khatri, and Mark Mikin. Thanks also to former *Esquire* editors David Katz and Brendan Vaughan.

THIS BOOK WAS PRODUCED BY

124 West 13th Street • New York, NY 10011 • www.melcher.com

Publisher: Charles Melcher • *Associate Publisher:* Bonnie Eldon • *Editor in Chief:* Duncan Bock

Executive Editor and Project Manager: Lia Ronnen • *Project Editor:* Lauren Nathan • *Production Director:* Kurt Andrews • *Production Assistant:* Daniel del Valle

Designed by Headcase Design: Paul Kepple, Ralph Geroni, Susan Van Horn
www.headcasedesign.com

Common Conversions

3 teaspoons = 1 tablespoon

2 tablespoons = ⅛ of a cup

4 tablespoons = 2 fluid ounces = ¼ cup

⅓ cup = 5 tablespoons + 1 teaspoon

½ cup = 4 fluid ounces = 8 tablespoons

¾ cup = 6 fluid ounces = 12 tablespoons

1 cup = 8 fluid ounces = 16 tablespoons

2 cups = 16 fluid ounces = 1 pint

4 cups = 1 quart

2 pints = 1 quart

4 quarts = 1 gallon

4 ounces = ¼ pound

8 ounces = ½ pound

16 ounces = 1 pound

1 jigger = 1½ ounces

1 dash = 2 pinches

1 pinch = three smidges

1 smidge = honestly, we have no idea